The StreetWise Guide to
BEING
ENTERPRISING

Increase Your Career, Business or Social Enterprise Prospects by using the E-Factor

David A. Gibson

Published by
OAK TREE PRESS
19 Rutland Street, Cork, Ireland
www.oaktreepress.com

A catalogue record of this book is
available from the British Library.

ISBN 978 1 904887 32-4

CONTENTS

PREFACE

Gordon Brown, then the UK Chancellor of the Exchequer, stated in 2002 that: "The education system's potential contribution to making Britain a more entrepreneurial society could be significant, but it is currently, neglected". Since that time, progress to promote the entrepreneurial society has still remained relatively slow. In particular, there is a need to develop further the enterprise behaviour and employability of students at all levels, not only to encourage small business start-ups but also to develop a culture of enterprise and innovation.

The National Commission on Entrepreneurship (2004) suggested that entrepreneurs have a range of personal characteristics, which include risk-taking, vision and confidence. Gibb (2002) also suggested that enterprise skills are very useful, not only in starting a business but also to enhance employment prospects. Thus, there has been a shift, both in the further and higher education enterprise curricula, to encourage students to develop "Enterprise for Life" skills that would be relevant and useful in self-employment, within a company or within social enterprise. The teaching of enterprise in further and higher education now is inextricably linked to both the enterprise and employability agenda of the government.

In many cases, the development of a business plan remains the basis for teaching and assessment within the enterprise curriculum. Although the development of the plan does provide some useful practice in the research and presentation of business information, there is a need for a greater focus on the underlying transferable skills that students will be able to use in the business life / career generally.

The StreetWise Guide to Being Enterprising and its companion **Work & Journal** provide a model that identifies a generic set of skills, designed to enable students to achieve success in business or career. These skills are analysed and their relevance to business and social enterprise are linked in a practical format.

Students, with the help of the E-Factor self-assessment questionnaire, will be able to identify areas of improvement in entrepreneurship, as well as to understand how to apply these skills in practice to develop a range of competencies. Practice in, and reflection on, the E-Factor skills provides the potential for students to become more entrepreneurial in whatever career they follow.

At policy level, it also may provide the base lever for a change in the enterprise culture and, ultimately, a more successful and entrepreneurial UK economy, through the creation of more global knowledge-based businesses, supported by entrepreneurial and innovative schools, colleges and universities.

This is a down-to-earth, readable, enjoyable and effective book that will appeal to students of all levels.

Professor Ken O'Neill BSc(Econ) Hon DSc ACMA FIBA MIoD
Holder of the Queen's Award for Enterprise Promotion – Lifetime Achievement Award

INTRODUCTION

Welcome to **The Streetwise Guide to Being Enterprising**, the first of a series of books to help people of all ages to be successful in any sphere of life.

To be enterprising is to create your own opportunities and to achieve your goals using the skills of an entrepreneur. In today's economic climate, it is up to us to make things happen for ourselves. Thankfully, there is a set of skills that you can learn which will enable you to move forward even in challenging times.

This book is based on my work with graduates and small businesses, in helping them to achieve "Enterprise for Life" skills. These tried and tested skills give you an opportunity to build on your subject knowledge, whatever it may be, and to make an impact on what is increasingly an international marketplace.

Enterprising people face the same challenges as the rest of us, whether in running their own business, a social enterprise or in a corporate setting. What enterprising people do differently is to turn problems into opportunities. This is how they make projects happen, and these successful projects in turn deliver which make both financial and social contributions, to the enterprisers and to society at large. Throughout the world, governments are realising that citizens must have innovation and enterprise competencies in addition to specific subject knowledge. They also know that being "streetwise" is important, so graduates of the future need commercial and social awareness on an international scale.

Please enjoy this book but, more importantly, please use it to develop your enterprise competencies. You must apply the knowledge and make it work for you. The most important concept to grasp is that you need to take responsibility for creating your own career.

Being an entrepreneur is not about necessarily about making millions; instead, it is about having a mindset, which is geared towards making a contribution, and the skills to turn opportunity into reality. I hope you will relate the book to your own circumstances.

Be enterprising and be in charge of your own life. Now, it is over to you. Get reading and, above all, start making things happen.

Professor David A Gibson
August 2009

1
INNOVATION & CREATIVITY

The key skills of an entrepreneur are his / her ability to spot opportunities, to create innovations, to solve problems and to find markets. In an era of rapid technological change, the ability to find innovative solutions is a key requirement whether you are in business or not. It is not enough to come up with a new idea for a product or project. In making the project happen, you will continue to have unforeseen problems. Can you continue to adapt and innovate to move the project forward, whatever the difficulty?

Organisations that have followed the same methods of operation for perhaps decades now have to "go with the flow" and adapt to change.

So, are you good at coming up with new ideas or do you find it difficult? It doesn't matter, you can improve your creativity. It is a skill like anything else – it just needs practice.

Let's do a little test. Have you ever written a poem, a song or appeared in a play? Have you ever drawn a picture? I defy you to say you have never done any of these activities. As a child, you are encouraged to use your imagination, to play games and to have fun. Once you reach the ages of 11/12, the education system tends to focus on developing your logical and analytical thinking. Unless you excel at art or music, there is little room in the curriculum for coming up with new ways to tackle things.

When I teach Creativity, I like to set the class a problem, usually involving coming up with new products or services to solve problems. For instance, the task might read: "In groups, outline five problems young people between 18 and 30 have and devise five new products or services to solve these".

Some of the students really struggle initially. They are not attuned to using creativity; gradually, however, they start having fun, generating silly ideas and start finding innovative solutions all over the place. The group dynamic helps, but also gradually the students start to believe that they could make a difference. When you realise you could come up with an idea that could make a difference, you start to look at ways of being enterprising and making the idea happen. It is amazing the change of attitude that takes place.

The problem always with training / teaching is that people forget to take the simple steps which can make the difference between applying their thoughts and turning knowledge into action. I usually get my students to sign an agreement to do three things and I want you to do the same now. If you keep this agreement for 30 days, you will increase your chance of being more innovative.

INNOVATION AGREEMENT

For the next 30 days, I _____ hereby promise to:

- Be more curious and look for unusual connections.
- Do a few things differently from normal each week.
- Buy a small notebook, take it everywhere for 30 days and write at least one new idea every day.
- Ask myself the following questions, every time I face a problem: What can I learn from this? What can I do to turn this around?
- Challenge normal solutions and not make assumptions about people or situations.

Signed _____

Date _____

If you are not prepared to sign this agreement, please do not read any more. This book is only for doers!

So let's start with a task!

TASK

Name five problems that young people aged 18-30 have. Find two new products and two new services that might solve one of these problems. Which is your best idea? If possible, do this with 2 friends.

INNOVATIONS & IDEAS

Getting started

Part of being innovative is an attitude of mind. Do you believe you can find new ways to do things? I hope you realise you can. It is simply being open to possibilities.

Look at some role models. Recently, I came across the story of a lady who found her son had run up a £500 monthly phone bill – on her phone! She worked in a video shop and was not a rocket-scientist. However, she knew she had a problem and was not sensible enough to realise she was too stupid to solve it. So, she came up with a rough design of a box unit that would block out certain numbers so that her son could not ring them. It was crude but effective – and six months later, it was available for sale at £30 in every B&Q in the UK – earning a small fortune for the lady in question.

What was so special about what she did? Not a lot. She had a problem and she tried to solve it. She used simple technology and her solution was basic. However, everyone who has a teenage son or daughter knows about screening calls and controlling phone bills. Everyone with teenagers will want to buy a unit. Simple solution, obvious market = success.

And, bear in mind that it is not just that a great idea could make you or your organisation a lot of money, your great idea could make a contribution to society way beyond its financial value – for instance, suppose you came up with a product or service that could benefit the community and donated the idea to a charity which could either raise money from it or use it to solve problems of their target group – that approach is just as enterprising as making money from the idea yourself.

In business, as in life in general, people are always trying to find solutions to challenges. To make a difference, you need to be prepared to think differently. Start by adopting a "what if" mindset.

So get going! Create one new idea a day from now on.

Case study

Let's look at a live case study. I'm sitting writing this chapter on a Sunday afternoon in May. Behind me, my teenage son is sitting at the computer. He is not interested in school. He is 15 and shows very little motivation. My wife and I have tried to explain to him how he needs to work harder at school if he wants to have a good career. I don't think we are getting through and neither are his teachers. The easy answer is to give up, let him learn his own lessons. How can I get across to him the consequences of not working at school and ending up with no qualifications?

The traditional answer locally is to get him to go to Church, join the Boy Scouts and do the Duke of Edinburgh Award, all of which he rejects. If he does not respond to that stereotype, what else can I do?

Since I am the person telling you to come up with innovative ideas, let's look at some solutions "outside the box". Is there a film he can watch? Is there a teenage TV programme that puts across this lesson? Who are his role models? What about a song or book or TV programme that tells their story but puts across the points that:

- Qualifications can open doors;

- You must work hard, if you want to achieve something.

How can I use texting, the internet, TV, his iPod, any of the media he uses to get information?

He has some interest in business and drama. How can I bring this alive, so that he can see what life would be like in these areas? How about inventing a game? Putting it on computer? How about a virtual reality business experience? How about setting up a competition? Using texting, etc., to stay in touch. How about a business thriller written by a teenager? How about a play in which he acts, based in a teenager starting a business?

You can see the ideas are starting to flow. I will keep you posted. If I can solve the problem, I reckon a lot of parents throughout the world would love to know my solution. So watch this space.

Is innovation a process?

There is a lot of argument as to whether you can follow a strict procedure – a process – to generate creative ideas or whether this goes against the whole idea of creativity, making random connections and "thinking outside the box". I think it would be rigid to exclude any method. You have to experiment to see what works for you. The most important thing is output, ideas that make a difference – how you arrive at them is less important.

As mentioned earlier, being curious, doing things differently and having a notebook to record random thoughts is a good start and is simple (buy a little notebook today and carry it with you everywhere – and I mean *everywhere*).

It would be remiss here not to discuss the work of the inventor of "lateral thinking", Edward De Bono. He believes that creativity is a process that can be taught at any level. He believes in the concept of "provocation", which is to challenge the traditional assumptions in any situation. If you join any organisation, from the Boy Scouts to a multinational company, you will quickly spot things that happen in a particular way "because that is the way we always do it". Believing that creativity is vital, as all organisations need to challenge themselves and be proactive in seeking improvement, de Bono devised a model – "the six thinking hats" – which encourages people to look at problems wearing different hats representing different problems.

The key to this is focus. If you have a problem, focus on it and solutions will come from the most unusual sources, partly because your subconscious mind is ticking away, thinking of connections, while you are doing something like sleeping or watching TV. This may lead to your "eureka" moment, like Archimedes in the bath. Personally, I have found some of my best ideas whilst out running.

De Bono comes up with various strategies to look at the problem from the outside. Another interesting strategy developed in Russia, from the study of major discoveries, is to "reverse", where you do the complete opposite of everything that has been done to date, as a model of change. Many times, this will give you a nonsense result – but, sometimes, it will open up new insights, which what innovation is all about.

Another popular model of innovation is the "Disney model", which uses techniques devised by Walt Disney. Basically, the Disney model involves being as creative as possible, suggesting any number of solutions. Then you criticise and try to pull them apart. Eventually, you try to pick the ideas that work best for you, which are creative but also make business sense. As you can imagine, the Disney model has a big focus on letting your imagination run riot to create lots of unusual possibilities and to make connections between contrasting areas by looking for the common ground.

Attitude

In innovating, it is important to have clearly defined goals and problems. Put simply, what it is you want to sort out? It is also important to have a good core belief like "there is always a way to sort things out". Otherwise, people or companies get too emotional about a problem, visualise the worst possible consequences and tend to "freeze" like a rabbit in headlights, even though the solution is obvious to a detached outsider.

Think back to times and situations when you have come up with a solution to what then seemed an impossible problem to other people.

Then try to find someone to model who is notorious for solving problems in an innovative way. Take a problem to them. Watch what they do, how they react, what processes they go through. You will probably find that they are relaxed, and have a strong belief that they will solve the problem (even before they know what the problem is!) and will have access to some good resources and lateral thinkers. Watch closely what they do. Copy them and you will find you will get a degree of their success.

Groups

There is no rule that you must work in groups in order to innovate. However, what other people contribute is a different perspective to your own. The ideal group suitable for "brainstorming" an idea are people with a diverse range of experience – the broader, the better. If you are a group of, say, six 25-year-old accountants or lawyers, I am not saying that you all will think exactly the same but you are unlikely to bring enough of a mix of experience to solve a problem that is proving too challenging for logical analytical thinkers, like accountants and lawyers. My suggestion is to create your own group of friends or co-workers who are as different as possible from each other, who meet on a regular basis to come up with new ideas and innovations.

I first came across this idea when I was presenting a Women's Enterprise programme. All of the participants on the programme had a business idea and all came from different backgrounds. There were lawyers, accountants, artists, housewives and teachers. We then took the idea of one of the participants and "brainstormed". The innovation flowed and every participant was left with much improved ideas, alternative markets and methods of operation. Why did it happen? First, there was a group dynamic, where everyone seemed to perform better as a team. The group had been given some time to gel and there were no major conflicts. However, the key to the success of the brainstorming session was the fact that everyone had different perspectives on the problem. The artist was able to help the lawyer and *vice versa*. This is a key input to innovation. Everyone has a different perspective and something to offer, if you are prepared to allow them time and space to make their contribution. It was amazing how the housewife could give the computer science graduate a perspective on how families and children use PCs and what were the important benefits to look for.

You may well work as part of a team or have a group of friends who hang around together. If the group is comfortable together that alone is a good start. However, also consider forming a specific "innovation group" with a range of people with diverse skills and background, all who have a common aim to produce ideas with commercial application. Ideally, you need the following mix to make a team successful: people who can think laterally; people who can share; people who perceive the problems and, last, a facilitator. Key elements to ensure the group's success include:

- Building of group rapport;
- Someone to lead and motivate the team;
- A process that the group likes to practice new ideas.
- Some form of motivation for the best idea.
- Someone in charge of follow-up / implementation of an idea.

It may take some time to find the right people for the group but time spending choosing wisely will pay dividends. And, although groups don't always come up with better ideas than lone thinkers, with the right group dynamic you will just watch those ideas flow.

Tony Buzan

Tony Buzan, the inventor of mindmaps, is another person who offers ideas and solutions to boost your creativity. His focus is on thinking and the brain. However, he has some surprisingly simple applications that you could apply to boost your creativity:

- Take breaks (I thought you might like this one!);
- Go for long walks;
- Be creative in your everyday life. He believes you can bring creativity into relationships, cooking and setting a table, for instance;
- Create your own imaginary mastermind group – a little weird, perhaps. Select people who you admire as resourceful and creative. They could be business people or politicians or even historical characters. When you have got a problem, ask them what you should do!
- Use Buzan's mindmapping process. This is a diagrammatic way of putting all your knowledge on a topic in diagrammatic fashion.

Let me do a mindmap for you for the E-Factor, starting with the title in the centre and showing a plan of the book (see **Figure 1.1**). Here goes! Mindmapping is simply a way of arranging your creative thoughts.

Buzan also suggests that you dance, sing, play music and draw. He believes in:

- Seeing things from different viewpoints;
- Making contributions.

Further, as we have suggested already, he believes that you should be curious like a child.

Figure 1 .1: The E-Factor mindmapped

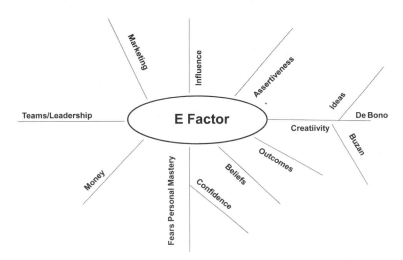

Conclusion

I am not saying that either de Bono or Buzan have it sussed. But, it is important to practice being creative and, if a structure helps you to do this, well and good. If not, do it anyway, and find what stimulates you. You may be like Archimedes and find the bath is the best place. The important thing is to have ideas — Linus Paul, the original developer of the Linux computer operating system, said that the best way to have a good idea is to have lots of ideas!

Equally important as having an idea is doing something with the idea. There are no marks for bright ideas that are not acted upon. That is another essential ingredient of the entrepreneur, the ability to take action. We will look at this later!

So let's summarise what we have learned.

Yes, you are a creative powerhouse. Your only problem is that you do not realise it yet. Innovation is a life skill from which anyone can benefit. Like all competencies, some of you will already have the skill at unconscious competence level already. That is, you are creative without thinking about it and are recognized as a very resourceful person, because you always come up with innovative solutions to problems. However, if you have spent 20 years as an engineer, practicing analytical thinking, you may have some work to do to use creativity in your everyday life. I hasten to add that I am not saying that you need to abandon all logic, just add creativity to your thinking skills to get the best results.

CREATIVITY

The creativity test

Have you ever come up with a new idea? Have you ever imagined the future? Have you ever done things differently? Have you ever solved a problem you were thinking about earlier as you drove along in the car or did something completely different? If so, you have been creative. Have you ever challenged an assumption about the way things are normally done? You have been innovative.

It is important that you **believe** you can come up with new ways of doing things. Honestly, it is half the battle. You are relaxed, you expect to find a solution and, because of this expectation, surprise, surprise, you do.

TASK 1.1

Make a commitment now that for the next 90 days you will practice being creative and looking for innovation.

Be curious and dare to fail

There are all sorts of people, circumstances and opportunities surrounding us every day. But, somehow, we all expect that, to find innovation, we have got to go to the USA or the Far East, maybe. The truth is that an innovation may be right in front of you. I don't know if you have ever heard the parable of the "acres of diamonds", where a man leaves home and spends his whole life searching for diamonds and dies in poverty without finding any. After his death, diamonds are found on his own ground. The moral of the story is to look around you and you will find your own acre of diamonds right there in your own life circumstances or contacts. Be prepared to be open and to look at opportunities that may not appear on first sight to amount to anything. As the founder of IBM, Thomas Watson, said, "Be prepared to fail more".

Dare to be different

The chances are that any innovation is likely to be something new and uncertain. As something new, it will meet opposition as many people and organisations, whatever their public profile, do not like change. Many of us (even those who write books about creativity and enterprise!) are creatures of habit. I find myself enjoying little routines. I like to set off for work at the same time, go the same route to the office, listen to the same radio show, park in the same space, go to the same café for breakfast and read the same newspaper. Bore of the year or what?

So I fight this. Some days, I go a different route, I read a different newspaper – I change everything. Why? If you keep doing the same things the same way all of the time, you keep getting the same results.

That is why innovation experts, such as Dr John Park of Robert Gordon University in Aberdeen, worry about too rigid processes / structures in coming up with ideas. The worry is that you will limit your range of innovative solutions, because you are sticking too rigidly to a routine. So, go out of your way to have new experiences, to travel to new places to get the stimulation you need. To innovate, you should be looking constantly for associations or connections between products, people and markets that have no obvious link.

For instance, mobile phones tend to be mainly the preserve of the young, with teenagers being particularly adept at using all the features, such as texting and ring tones. Elderly people, as a group (though not all), are not as comfortable with new technology, many don't own mobile phones and those who do shy away from using them too much. However, recently, when explaining new ideas in a workshop with 300 nurses, I explored the health and social problems of the elderly. The nurses identified many different problems, including the difficulty of the elderly in communicating with the outside world and their inability to use the simplest technology that could help significantly with their safety, health and other personal and social issues. When the group brainstormed, they came up with a new mobile phone with just a few basic keys to press, less of a toy and more a simple device that would meet the needs of the elderly for instant communication.

And, just to show that great minds think alike, a week later, mobile phone operator O_2 announced that it was designing such a product.

TASK 1.2

Set yourself a daily creativity goal. Buy yourself a small notebook and write one idea in it every day. Carry it with you everywhere.

The point I am trying to get across is that idea generation is not just something you do to find a new product or a solution to a specific problem. It is something you should do continually, since you will find you will have to continually innovate as a project is implemented.

Daydream

Like me, you may have been told many times, at school and at home, not to daydream. However, using your imagination, visualising situations and unusual connections is a great way to stimulate creativity. Einstein arrived at his famous theory of relativity while imagining travelling on a time machine back and forward in timelines.

A proven technique that you may want to try when you have got a goal or challenge is to visualise yourself having achieved the end result and then to work back to see what stages you have gone through to get to that end result. Again, you have "fooled" your mind that you have arrived at the end result; your subconscious will not recognise the difference and is likely to show the pathway to the end result, something that a logical planning process will have difficulty in arriving at.

Competitive advantage

Again, unless you are lucky enough to be setting up a business or to be working for an organization that has unlimited resources, you need innovation as your competitive advantage to compete with the "big boys". You may not have the money to devise a traditional marketing strategy but instead you will have to adapt "guerrilla" strategies, simple and cheap marketing plans that can help you reach the customer without traditional levels of advertising and expenditure.

So where do ideas come from?

Ideas can come from anywhere. You can find an idea simply by listening respectfully to anyone. As far as I am concerned, one of the most innovative businesses of recent years was "The Big Issue". The owner listened to the need for many people trying to re-establish themselves on the work ladder to earn money independently and funded a very successful business, which is also a strong social enterprise.

Market trends
The press and market reports will let you know major trends. What are the trends of today? A vastly increased aging population; the power of the mobile phone as a communications tool; the opening up of international trade borders; the economic growth of China and India; the list is endless. There are unlimited ideas from these trends alone.

A personal problem
What really pisses you off? Chances are it pisses a lot of other people off, too. Solve the problem and you have a potential idea.

Technology
Innovation is about an attitude of mind that you must bring to your future work / life pursuits.

For example, technology is developing at an increasingly fast rate, speeding up most processes up and adding value, in many cases. However, technology is not always the answer. Technologically-innovative products can take 10 years or more to devise, but maybe the simple use of more basic technology can solve the problem now and make a significant impact.

Different industries
Businesses and social organisations operate differently. How an airplane manufacturer markets its product will be very different from how financial services are marketed. How staff are treated in universities may differ significantly from how staff in a manufacturing plant are handled, and so on. What would happen if you transferred some of the learning strategies from one industry to another? In some cases, it would transform an industry's results – perhaps for the better. For instance, lawyers tend to adopt a fairly narrow range of marketing strategies, many relying on their reputation and

long-standing professional relationships. But, if you were a newly-formed legal practice, yet to establish a reputation, how would you establish market share? How about looking at how companies in intensely competitive sales environments operate? If you took those strategies, customised them and ensured there was nothing that clashed with professional guidelines, your innovation could make a substantial and lasting impact (to your bottom line!).

Association connection searching

As discussed, new connections between different areas can produce innovation. So, you need to search constantly for these connections.

De Bono, Buzan and many of the other creativity gurus all have created tools to stimulate connection-making. For instance, there is a random word game that encourages you to take three words to build crazy connections and then take the ideas from there.

Let's do this, taking three random words that occur to me now as I write:

- McDonalds (I am writing this in a branch of the great "health food" chain!);

- Pets (I was thinking of my cat – sad, I know);

- Enterprise (I spend my life encouraging people to be more enterprising and helping businesses and organisations to be more entrepreneurial and create results).

Here we go:

- "McDonalds" for pets;

- A pet franchise organisation;

- A place to keep pets outside any food store;

- A promotion scheme for McDonalds to provide money for pet sanctuaries;

- Pet franchises as businesses – grooming, psychology, pet hotels, etc.

- Establish pet products with a new brand name;

- Creativity classes for pet owners;

- Use animal skills behaviours as a way of teaching people to be enterprising;

- Marketing links between pet skills and McDonalds;
- A social enterprise to promote a worldwide pet club promoted through McDonalds;
- Use the McDonalds child-friendly marketing strategies to market pets;
- Learn business skills through pet handling;
- Pure vegetarian McDonalds;
- McDonalds' staff training – customers as pets;
- Pet service units set up to be as efficient as a McDonalds;
- A pet as a new children's character to replace Ronald McDonald;
- Pet products for school enterprise projects;
- McDonalds pet food shops.

Some very wacky ideas, I know, but I just wanted to illustrate the process openly and honestly. Some of these are completely useless ideas but some have connections that might be worth taking forward – watch out for the new pet McDonalds character coming to a store near you! And, a week after doing this exercise, I spotted a success book based on sheepdog strategies – weird or what?

You are likely to achieve the best results if you practice creativity on an ongoing basis, if you get other people involved who can provide different perspectives and market knowledge, and where you are motivated to solve a particular problem. Without taking time to practice, you will not improve this significant E-Factor.

But, on its own, it is only half of the equation for the enterprising person. There are many great ideas people, who are not necessarily successful business people. However, the creation of a new idea can transform lives, and not only that of the idea-generator. Life is a constant challenge; identifying solutions that provide significant commercial or community opportunity is a worthwhile contribution. Make sure you do your bit.

What makes a good idea?

Hopefully, now you are a creativity powerhouse, bursting with ideas – well, at least, you have one idea that you hope might work. How do you know if it is a good idea or not?

In my view, a good idea will have a clear market, will make some use of technology, ideally will have some international potential and will be capable of being protected by a patent. It also makes life easier if you do not require years of research or huge finance, even if, on a cost-benefit analysis, the long term market for your research / finance-intensive product suggests that your idea is feasible.

It also depends what you want from your idea or creative thought. You may simply want to deal with the challenge your local Help the Aged store faces and have no interest in making a more significant contribution. However, my argument is that, as an enterprising person, your wish to have wider impact can lead to greater financial reward or contribution for you, the business you work for, or the community organisation or charity you nominate to benefit from your innovation.

A key point is that your idea might be the greatest technical innovation ever but, if no one wants it, it is likely to disappear without a trace.

Note that, if your idea can be copied and you can't protect your ownership of it, you are likely to lose it. Some ideas are "me too" and, because they lack innovative content, you will lose any competitive advantage unless you build in some innovative way of doing things into the venture.

Sadly, some good ideas also will be stolen. A new invention with market potential is worth a significant sum of money and you need to contact the Patent Office as soon as possible to see if you can protect it. The good news is that if you can, and it has market potential, there is likely to be some help from enterprise support agencies to pay part of the cost of protection. Trademarks, logos, designs and copyright also all provide some form of cover. Perhaps one of the easiest protections is to get anyone you talk to about your innovation to sign a non-disclosure agreement before you discuss it in detail.

Having once taught a female participant on an Enterprise course for three months without ever knowing her idea, and therefore finding it hard to help develop it, I sometimes find people to be overly secretive but there is no use denying it, there are some sharks out there. Ask Dyson of vacuum cleaner fame, who spent 10 years fighting to protect his patent. It would be unfair to make you think that once you have a patent, no one will trouble you. There are plenty of major companies that will test your capacity and finances for a long legal fight; the involvement of a university or major sponsor can help in protecting your idea.

But, the reality is that getting to market as quickly as possible, and capturing a significant market share before your competitors can react, probably is your greatest protection of the intellectual property in your idea.

Commercialising your idea

It is important that, once you have generated a new idea you want to implement, you do some assessment work.

The first thing is to assess the resources to make it happen. Have you got access to money, market intelligence, networking, and prototype and product development help? Who can provide it? You will find enterprise support or regional development agencies very helpful here. Not only have they got staff and resources to help but they are constantly searching to promote "global businesses" in their areas. Any product or service with international potential becomes a possible economic contribution to the region.

You also need to self-assess. Have you got some commercial skills? Can you make it happen, and are you willing to develop yourself along with the product? Some business people, like Sir Alan Sugar, for instance, seem to have the creative capacity to develop products, the ability to make things happen and the influence to get results. But many people, particularly those in academic and technical functions, can develop the idea but are then deficient in any of the other E-Factor skills.

The whole message of this book is that you can develop your competencies in all the E-Factor skills. However, although significant development is possible if you are willing to learn and apply the necessary techniques, or if you are very creative but lack some of the other qualities, it can be sound business practice to bring other entrepreneurs into your team or, in some cases, to consider licensing others to use your product rather than developing it yourself. If need be, enlist the help of independent advisers to assess the best options.

However, I strongly believe that whatever you prefer to do – create or implement – you should work on the other half of the equation, even if only to appreciate what is being done. If not, the innovators may change the product you make, or the business people may attempt to "wipe your eye". If in doubt, read my other book, **The Streetwise Guide to Starting Your Own Business**, to learn some of the business realities, so that you can ask the right questions and thus make the right decisions.

If you work somewhere, who owns the idea?

If you are working for a company and you develop an innovation, be very clear about who owns the rights. Most employment contracts state that anything invented in company time belongs to the company; some go as far as saying that anything invented while you are an employee, whether on or off the premises, belongs to the company. If in doubt, get independent legal advice. Some innovators don't care about the financial rewards for their innovations – for example, Tim Berners Lee, the inventor of the Internet, arguably the most significant innovation of the past 50 years, has achieved little financial reward from his creativity. There is nothing wrong with this; it depends on your motivation. Just make sure you get what you want, as intellectual property can be very valuable.

Be innovative or die!

A bit of a dramatic statement but long gone are the days where individual companies and the public sector could afford to "rest on their laurels". There is constant change, global competition and continuous technological development everywhere. If an organisation or an individual does not respond to this, they are likely to be left behind.

Innovation is an attitude of mind. Even when you have a good product or service, you need to focus your attention on certain types of questions. Does this product or service need to change to meet client needs? How can I improve my contribution to the client? What do we need to do now to take this forward?

Depending on your business or job, you may not be allowed to experiment on actual customers with new procedures and processes in the search for innovation. For example, if you are a doctor, you will be required to follow certain pre-determined procedures to ensure the health and safety of your patient. However, that does not mean that you should not be open to new ideas or new solutions to problems that your patients have that are not being met by the current procedures. And, if you want to lead, you should be looking always to find new ways to help staff use resources most effectively and efficiently and to ensure you and your colleagues are the best you can be.

Am I expected to be creative?

Yes. Obviously, if you are starting a new business, you will be searching for a new idea and will be forced to be innovative to survive, as conditions and markets constantly change. Those of you going into professions will find that you are expected to innovate and contribute creatively, as professions and their professional bodies demand that you have to adapt to ongoing changes. And in business in general – and even in the public sector or non-profit world, change is constant and so creativity is demanded. So, yes, you are expected to be creative – start practising now!

Can I do it?

I have tried to tell you constantly that you **can** do it. The first pre-condition is that you should want to do it and that you are convinced that you must, otherwise you will self-sabotage. Second, you must practice it in real life.

I am about to set you a task which I want you to complete and return to me by email within the next 30 days. Why I am doing this? Because I passionately believe there is a strong difference between knowing what to do and actually doing it. You need creativity and innovation to become one of your competencies, just like driving, which most of you probably do now without any conscious thought. To reach that stage, you will have to go through stages of practising it, getting it wrong, getting sabotaged by others, get to the stage of making good progress by persisting and finally doing it as part of your normal, everyday range of behaviours. It will take persistence, commitment and the willingness to learn but, above all, it will take action.

It is up to you to decide whether you are happy simply to be aware of the growing importance of creativity and innovation or whether you want to use some of it to be more enterprising and to improve some aspect of your work or life situations. As always, it is up to you. If I were your personal coach, I would be there to motivate you and cajole you every day. If you need this help, find someone who is prepared to help you.

Although this book contains eight separate E-Factors, I believe that creativity is the most important (hence its place at the start of the book), as I believe that identifying opportunities and then making them happen are the key enterprise qualities that not only any budding entrepreneur should have, but also anyone who wants to be personally excellent in whatever their choice of career or community volunteering.

I promise you that not only will you perform better in work / enterprise but the same qualities can also improve your personal / family life.

Now, it is time to complete the task. You are not allowed to move onto the next chapter until you do so!

TASK 1.3

A large American multinational company has recruited you as its "Innovation Trainee" on £50,000 per annum. You have been set the following tasks and must provide a 500-word report to the managing director within 30 days with your answers:

- Identify 10 problems/challenges that teenagers have.

- Come up with five new products and five services that will help them.

- Pick your best idea and explain your reasons.

- Outline the first four things you would do to take your idea forward.

- Explain what you will do every day to become a more creative person.

2

SELF-MANAGEMENT

Starting your own business or developing a successful corporate or community enterprise should be straightforward. You read a "how to" manual (like my **Streetwise Guide to Starting Your Own Business**), you achieve your goals, become rich and famous and live happily ever after. Yet this scenario rarely happens, because possibly your biggest problem will be yourself. We all know what we should do and yet we don't do it.

Why?

We all have difficulty in taking action and doing the right thing. The ability to control our emotions and win the "inner game" with ourselves is very important. We all have a psychological make-up and have been programmed by our life experience to date. Your performance in your career or business or life in general depends on your beliefs, focus, self-esteem, confidence and ability to control your emotions.

We are creatures of habit. If you have been programmed by life experiences and your family over the past 20 years that "you lack confidence", or that you are "useless at anything practical", you will tend to believe what you are told and will have ingrained these attitudes in your habits. The longer this goes on (those of you who, like the author are over 35, pay attention), the more challenging it is to break free from that mindset. It is a bit like going under in a swimming pool, you will have to make a tremendous effort to escape your previous programming. The question is whether you can change your make-up – or, indeed, whether you want to. The problem is that, unless you do change, you will hold yourself back from being the best you can be.

Can you change?

Of course, you can. People change habits all the time. They get into a different environment or find some reason strong enough to get them to act differently. Have you ever met a bride-to-be who had not slimmed before her "big day"? I have met several men with chronic smoking and exercise habits, who, after a stroke, when their life prognosis if they didn't change their habits was spelt out to them, changed their habits quite remarkably. It is a pity, though, that it has take a life or death experience (I don't mean marriage!) to get us to change.

You need to use some of the principles I will explain to you in this chapter to help bring about the change you desire. However, first, you have to want to change. Other people may suggest the changes as good strategy but you have to want it yourself. If you remember the old series of "lightbulb" jokes – how many (name a profession) does it take to change a lightbulb? – the answer for psychologists was "only one, but the lightbulb has to really want to change"! So do you.

And, counter-intuitively, research has shown it is easier to make big changes in your outlook or beliefs, which can then lead on to several smaller changes, than to start with small changes and work up.

BELIEFS & VALUES

Your beliefs play a fundamental part in your success / performance. If you start a new project where there is a degree of uncertainty, there are plenty of people who will forecast its failure, simply because it is new and untested. You need to have a strong belief in yourself and your project to overcome this negativity. This is a key selling point for any potential suppliers / customers / investors.

I come from Northern Ireland where people are natural pessimists. There is nothing wrong with some degree of realism or preparation against unexpected events. However, you will need strong belief if you are to keep going when you meet the inevitable setbacks. The power of belief in business and support is illustrated in the survival of West Bromwich Albion in the Premiership football league. Each year, at Christmas, the team at the bottom of the league would be relegated. In the 2004/5 season, the bottom team was West Bromwich, led by their new manager Bryan Robson, a great ex-footballer with an indifferent managerial career and no wins in his first 12 league matches. Somehow, he managed to instil a belief in the team that they could survive and break all the unwritten rules.

Case study

One of my clients, Samuel, got involved in a get-rich-quick venture that was doomed to failure. He was almost "brainwashed" by his associates into believing that the project would work. Needless to say, it failed, through no fault of Samuel's. Having always succeeded in life where he had put in hard work, either as a child or adult, this affected him badly. Later, he started a new business, presenting business seminars since he had a talent for presentation. However, every time when things started to go wrong with a seminar, he literally gave up. It was almost as if he was looking for the excuse to bolster his new belief that "nothing ever works for me". This was ironic because, as part of his job, Samuel was involved in recruiting participants for seminars and was always successful. Obviously, this situation required urgent attention. Let me tell you some of the things we did to challenge this.

I spent some time with Samuel, talking over the three recruitment drives for seminars where he had quit. On each occasion, when something went wrong, he explained that "I just felt it wasn't going to work out". I started to test his belief. The conversation went like this:

"Have you ever run a successful course?", I asked.

Yes, he had.

"What would happen if you kept going, whatever the problems?".

"I might fail", he said.

"Would that be so bad?".

"No".

"Just because one business venture failed, does that mean you will always be a failure?".

"My wife thinks so".

"What do you think?".

"I don't know".

"What if I said you would get £5,000, if you could show me you gave everything to recruiting for the seminar, whatever the result?"

He smiled, "I guess I would really go for it".

"Why don't you take this attitude?"

So, I asked him to visualise a successful recruitment drive for a seminar, finding it easy to get new participants and the seminar itself working out as a great success. I told him to do it twice a day for five minutes. I wanted him to do this for 30 days. He did as he was asked and I believe this was a factor in boosting his belief and ability to take action. Your subconscious mind responds to images, sounds and feelings. If you continually visualise your outcome, you go a long way towards convincing yourself that it will actually happen. It's something that sports people do as part of their training routine.

Get a set of empowering beliefs

No one can confirm whether a belief is true or not. People sometimes have very strong self-delusional beliefs that can lead to irrational actions. For instance, there are some fundamental religious beliefs, where the "believers" feel they must impose the death penalty on non-believers. Not very rational, from most people's point-of-view but entirely sensible to the "believers". However, you can see that beliefs which inspire you can play an important part in helping you achieve your goals.

Here are some beliefs that I have found useful. I read them every day and I am constantly looking for examples that show these beliefs to be true.

1   There is always a way.

2   I can make this happen.

3   I can be whatever I want to be.

4   There are opportunities everywhere.

5   I love the challenge of business.

6   I believe I can make a contribution to the world.

7   I can be a millionaire.

8   No matter what the problem, I can turn it around.

9   There is no failure, only feedback.

10 Money and opportunity are attracted to me.

TASK 2.2

Write out these beliefs – or amend them to include some of your own – and put the page somewhere where you will see it and can read it everyday. Make it a habit of yours to read this page of beliefs every day.

Obviously, a track record of success helps anyone to build strong self-belief. If you did well at school and were in the first rugby team, you would have been considered a success – you will believe that you will do well and will act confidently until something major happens in your life to contradict this. If your performance at school or in life generally was less stellar, then you probably need to work on your self-belief – most of us do!

Be your own coach

There will be times when the whole world seems to be against you. If, like Samuel above, you lose all your money, you will suffer from the vagaries of human nature. People will turn on you and will perceive you as a failure. This is part of our culture, whereas in the USA someone who has had a go, albeit unsuccessfully, is perceived as the type of person who will succeed on their next attempt (and they will be allowed another attempt), provided they learn from their mistakes.

It can help to have someone to believe in you when perhaps you are at your lowest ebb and you start to doubt yourself. Samuel tried hard, picked a poor opportunity and failed in it. As a result, business associates, family and friends saw him as a person who was no good at business. What was ironic was that some of the doubters had never actually tried any type of business venture themselves. In those circumstances, unquestioned support and the ability to show the belief that "the past does not equal the future" is paramount for success. We all need mentors who believe in us.

Action planning

There is an entire chapter of this book (**Chapter 8**) devoted to being action-orientated – it's that important.

For now, it's enough to understand that taking small action steps not only helps you to achieve your goals, but also helps you to build belief in yourself as each milestone is reached. As you tackle a situation and establish a small success, build on that for the future. Strong beliefs and values help to set out where you want to go.

Instead of replaying over in your mind situations that went wrong, remember when you achieved something you thought impossible. Remember the people who do believe in you. Seek out role models of people who have turned things round and achieved the seemingly impossible. What did they say? What did they do? Why did they believe in themselves?

A four-stage approach

The type of belief I want you to have is a belief in your capabilities, with the ability to visualise yourself achieving the end result. However I do want you to retain some flexibility, particularly with regard to strategy. You may have the capabilities and the opportunity to make things happen but there is always the possibility that your present way of making a project happen is not working, no matter what your self-belief.

You need to adapt a four-stage approach to being a success, which underpins a lot of the strategy in this chapter. The stages are:

- Know what you want.
- Take action.
- Be very aware of the results you are getting.
- If you are not getting the results you want, change and take a new approach to make things happen.

Belief is challenging when you start off, because of the reaction you will get from others who are negative about new situations. If you have done your homework, you need self-belief and a belief in your project. I have no doubt that you have excellent potential and are capable of making things happen. However, you need to transmit this belief in your capability to other people because they will judge your venture and decide whether they will back it with reference to two factors: the competitive advantage of the idea and your capabilities.

There are lots of clichés from the world of positive thinking but it is true that "what you believe you can achieve". Always believe in yourself, but be prepared to learn, adapt, innovate and, if necessary, change course. Belief always needs to be backed up by appropriate action. If you have a vision for the long-term, that's great as it will help you with your decisions along the way. It can also be useful in achieving small goals step-by-step, and the actual achievement will build your belief further. Ultimately your beliefs are a self-fulfilling prophecy. To quote Henry Ford, "If you believe you can, you are right. If you believe you can't, you are right. It is up to you".

TASK 2.3

What is one new belief you will now use? Do it now!

Values

It is important first of all to know what your values are and to make sure your projects / businesses / career are in line with those values. If you are anti-war, it does not make a lot of sense to work for the Ministry of Defence. But if you believe strongly in ethical trade, working for a Fairtrade company will be a pleasant experience. When the project / business and your values are aligned, the chances of successful outcomes are increased.

TASK 2.4

Put the following list of values into order of preference with your highest first: freedom, security, money, health, family, integrity spirituality.

Give yourself five minutes to do this.

How did you do? What was first? There is no right or wrong answer. Is health right up high on your list? If security is your most important value, should you be starting a business in this age of financial uncertainty? If money is very high up, are you working in a career or business that will lead to the financial success you crave? How about if you shifted your values, could that have a positive impact on your performance /contribution? In his book, based on the hit TV series, *The Apprentice*, Sir Alan Sugar made it crystal clear what was his number one value: family always before business. Yet he seems to have done OK. There are many people who put money first, before health or family, etc. Health should be high up, simply because to remain the enterprising individual you already are, you need a high level of energy and good health. When family, relationships and health are prioritised, there is less likely to be a conflict and you can focus on achieving the task in hand.

However, do what you feel is right for you. If you achieve short-term success in a lucrative venture but which is contrary to your values and beliefs, there is always going to be a conflict, which may spill-over into other areas of your life.

MOTIVATION

In making anything happen, the **why** is very often more important than the **how**. When we talk of leadership (**Chapter 7**), we will consider the importance of motivating others. However, an enterprising person, whenever and wherever they operate, is essentially a self-starter, who will do whatever it takes because of their own high level of self-motivation.

Your motivation obviously will be helped if you are doing what you love and are good at and if you believe strongly in what you are doing. However, many projects flounder, because the challenge is to remain motivated when there seems to be a lack of immediate results or something else intrudes.

Pain or pleasure

People often are motivated by either pain or pleasure. They will take the appropriate action when either they wish to avoid something negative happening or where some appropriate type of reinforcement reward could happen. Which works for you? Or is it both? I certainly like to get tangible rewards, financial or otherwise, for what I do. However, avoidance of major pain seems to be a key driver to get me to take action.

How do I use this?
Suppose you want to make a major change, let us say to become more financially successful. You know there are strategies that will help but you never seem to get around to implementing them. For instance, three key strategies that could lead to long-term financial success would be buying investment property, building up a pension fund, and starting a lucrative business.

My suggestion is: imagine yourself in 20 years time; you never got motivated and you still haven't done anything about the key financial strategies. What would your life be like? How would you feel? Imagine your lifestyle. If you visualise this in detail and turn up the pressure, you will begin to feel the pain. No pension, no life insurance, no private medical care, no money to support your family, no self-respect, no chance to retire or make a contribution – just huge regrets and recriminations.

However, if reward is what motivates you, imagine instead the benefits you will have if you take action now and work to achieve those financial goals. Imagine no work, time to indulge in lengthy holidays, no financial worries, the ability to help family and friends financially, good healthcare, freedom to travel, to go where you want and do what you want – an ideal life.

It is also important to do this on a short-term basis, because the achievement of any long-term goal is based on a large number of small steps. Management guru, Peter Drucker, once explained that, "long-range planning does not deal with future decisions, but with the future of present decisions". It is important, therefore, that you find your "hot button". What is it that will get you moving?

In selling, people often have great difficulty in achieving a sale, as to get one sale, they need to get 10 sales interviews; to get 10 interviews, they may have to contact 100 prospects. If you need 100 prospects to get one sale, how do you motivate yourself for the 99 rejections along the way? Simple, work out what the value of one sale is. Let us say it is £1,000. So, each of the 100 calls is worth £10 and each "No" is another £10 on the way to achieving the goal of the £1,000 sale. You need to find your why in every project and use that to motivate yourself when times get tough.

Again, it could be useful for you to do some simple psychometric tests to help evaluate what motivates you. Talking to family and friends will also help.

People who set goals and have a mission will often have a "scrapbook" with pictures of the end goal or some means of bringing this alive. Let us say that what you want most of all is a lovely home in the countryside. Looking at the goals and the visual images once a day will hep you realise why you are having all this hassle. Beliefs and values will play a part, too. In his book on values, Hyrum Smith poses this test: If you agreed to risk your own life crossing a plank 200 yards long to save the person at the other end, who would that person be? Your answer may surprise you. Dramatic, I know, but an effective way of identifying motivation.

The principle of delayed gratification is a useful reminder, that you should not always expect immediate rewards and that you always need to have your strategic vision to hand as the capacity to act now for long term benefits is something you must master. However, find simple ways of relaxing yourself for action in the short-term – perhaps a hot bath, reading a book, a walk, etc, whatever helps you.

Control your emotions

We are all at the mercy of our emotions to a lesser or greater extent. Without wanting to turn you into a machine, you should not let emotions control you completely, particularly in business.

Sensitivity

The right type of sensitivity is a good asset in business. Being able to read people and situations and being sensitive to the needs of others can be important for marketing. However, being oversensitive to the opinions of others, and easily hurt, will not help. We are not always able to choose what life throws at us. I do believe, however, that we ultimately determine our destiny, but sometimes we are thrown some key situations and challenges which do not obviously appear helpful. All you can work on is your reaction to events, and try to turn them round to the advantage of yourself or others.

One of the most inspirational one-liners I heard recently was from James Boddy, a businessman and philanthropist, on addressing a group of students, "Whatever life throws at you, get the champagne out". It is not always easy to see the joy in some scenarios that will appear. However, you will have a better chance of working with them, if you have a positive attitude and realise it is part of your journey / test and that you must embrace it and move on with your life. I was particularly impressed by two motivational speakers I heard recently. One had had a leg and a hand blown off in Mozambique whilst working for a mines removal agency. His story of how he searched for his arm / leg and his relief on realising he had something left, including his "credentials", was hilarious. If he can react this way, why can't you? Mark Pollack, who is blind, adopts the same attitude. Both men continue to challenge themselves physically, to inspire other people to face obstacles, and to refuse to be beaten. From somewhere, they have got a focus we should all take when dealing with challenges. Ask yourself positive focus questions, "What is good about this? What can I learn from this so I can help others? What can I do to turn this to my / our advantage?".

Controlling state

You all know there are certain times when you feel more powerful and are more likely to achieve results. I believe that physiology plays a part. How are you standing? Are you smiling? What is your body language? Can you change it?

Relaxation
Your capacity to be enterprising is increased if you can learn to be relaxed. This may seem to be in direct contradiction to many small business courses quite often presented by an employee of a local enterprise agency who has never run their own business. They like to advise, "For the first five years of your business, you must work 25 hours a day. You can never relax!". Absolute rubbish. The first skill you should learn is to relax and to make time for it. This helps you deal less emotionally with life's trials.

I don't know if you have ever met someone who practices meditation on a regular basis. Their very presence relaxes you. I read a profile last night of Brian Turtle, Director of BIFHE, one of the top three FE colleges in the UK. He explained how he enjoys his work and doesn't worry. If he can relax with the massive financial and business challenges he faces, so can you.

The only time you are taught how to relax in this country is when you have a baby. Yet I believe it is the ultimate skill for business. I think we all realise that momentum is important in business. However, relaxed focus can help an individual to concentrate on key issues to bypass stress and to make more effective decisions.

TASK 2.5

Find a class or tape that teaches relaxation. It could be meditation, deep relaxation or self-hypnosis. Practice 15 minutes every day.

Also spend five minutes every day practising quick relaxation, learning to relax muscles and focus on receiving bad news.

This 15-20 minutes every day could change your life. It is also ideal to be in a relaxed state should you want to visualise the achievement of future goals or habit change. Being relaxed helps you visualise with your right brain and stops the incessant analysis and chatter which gets in the way.

FEARS

We are driven by our fears and, although you can't get rid of them completely, you must not let them get in the way of your goals. It is right to be afraid of dangerous animals, dangerous road conditions and serious illness. What you have to work on are the irrational fears that hold you back. If we are scared of something, our natural reaction is to avoid whatever is causing the fear. People become so skilled at this avoidance that they can end up keeping away from some of the important things in life, such as relationships.

Irrational fears can be very extreme, after some particularly bad experiences and can almost turn into a "phobia". If you have a fear this extreme, you may need to get some professional help.

However you can improve your ability to cope with fears through a number of approaches. Find out what works for you.

Fear will always be there

A lot of approaches get us to accept that the fear is not going away, to accept it but to go ahead and to do what you have to do. A lot of seminar leaders will get you to do something you never thought possible, like walking on fire. Having found that, under the right conditions, this was possible to do, then you should let go of your fears from now on.

Have you any fears?

Have you any underlying fears that could hold you back? At least, admit them to yourself. A few of the key fears that hold you back in enterprise where you need to take risks are fear of failure and fear of rejection. Statistics show these are very significant fears that tend to inhibit someone's capability to take action.

You will need to work with fear if you are going to achieve any significant success. We will discuss this further when we look at personal influence. You will face "No"s, even if you are only asking for people to help you. If you take these "No"s personally, you will quietly become inhibited. Searching for team members, looking for help and selling are all examples where not everything you do will work. As Thomas Watson, founder of IBM, advised, "You need to fail more often". School does not prepare us to fail, and yet that is how you will learn, not only in sales but at every stage of your venture project. You do not know who is going to help, who is going to hinder and who is going to help you achieve results. So, you have to be relaxed, as to both rejection and failure, since in bringing an innovation to life, there will be plenty of both. That is where someone who has some type of direct sales experience has an advantage, simply through being relaxed about the fact that not every one will support you or everyone will agree with you.

Geoff Thompson, an ex-martial artist who became an author and a playwright, used his own version of "systematic desensitisation", where you grade your fears and gradually work your way through them, achieving success at every step. If you are scared to make a presentation to the board of directors of a company, for instance, start by presenting to a friend, and then perhaps a small presentation to a group of colleagues, gradually reaching a more challenging audience until you are ready for the board. Sometimes, you may be ready to "jump in at the deep end" and, although this type of approach can be very successful, you have to be prepared sometimes for it to go wrong and then to learn from it.

Geoff Thompson's greatest fear was physical confrontation. To overcome it, he became a nightclub bouncer and had to deal with it and overcome the fear. However, I don't think you need to do anything quite so drastic!!

If you have identified what is the real fear holding you back, you are halfway there. Work on your fear, tackle it step-by-step. Every attempt, no matter how small, is a major step forward.

In my youth, I had a very severe fear of speaking in public after a particularly unsuccessful "mock court debate" in my first year at University. I spent about three years successfully avoiding speaking in front of a group again. Suddenly, I was asked to take a one-off class at a FE college. I had no choice and was not happy about doing so. However, the girls, final year A level students, were friendly and quite undemanding. I started to believe I could do it and, today, speaking in public holds no fears for me. If an idiot like me can do it, so can anyone!!

Confidence and self-esteem

You need to learn to like yourself. Again, it comes down to programming. If you lack confidence, it is not because you were born that way, it has a lot to do with environment. Many of us come from well-meaning families who did not want us to get above ourselves as children. This can lead to a lack of confidence in our own abilities. You need to realise that you have talents and that you have every right to be confident in doing something you have experience or ability at. Affirmations can prove useful. "I like myself" is a very simple affirmation but effective. "I can and I will" is another example of an affirmation that should be repeated on an ongoing basis.

A useful ploy, when carrying out a task that you do not feel confident about, is to act as if you are. You will act differently and get a different reaction from your audience. The ironic thing is that, by moving differently and acting out this role, and achieving at least some success, you will start to feel more confident yourself.

It is nice to have some cheerleaders in your life. I don't mean in the literal sense! I am thinking of people who will encourage you. You need to be careful as to who you share your hopes and dreams with. It could be a member of your family, a friend or a mentor at work.

Visualisation can also be a useful strategy. In your daily relaxation session, imagine yourself as more confident, acting confidently, being the person you want to be. If you could do this for just five minutes every day, your confidence levels would soar.

You also must monitor your self-talk. If you have this little voice inside your head that tells you every time you do something wrong, "You are useless", you need to change this. Again, change your focus to "How can I do better next time?".

Learn to respect yourself, to treat yourself just as you would a friend you were trying to encourage and help develop, so you can see not only do you have to master communication with the outside world, you have to work on it yourself.

Be careful of the words you use. Let us say that you forgot to tax your car yesterday, when it was due for renewal. "This is a nightmare" is inappropriate use of language. It's not a "nightmare", it's a mistake and one that's easily fixable at that.

Work on the memories you want to enhance and let go those you want to forget. Remember a time when you were a big success. Feel yourself there, create the sounds and the feeling to leave a positive association. If you have had an experience that haunts you and dents your confidence, see it as a distant picture with yourself in it, keeping the image dull and lifeless – and free of any emotion. This is to stop the habit we all tend to have of reliving bad memories.

A final strategy can be to remember a time when you acted confidently and were in a good state of mind. Find something visual or a piece of music that you associate with that occasion. Anytime you want to recapture that feeling, find something visually similar, some similar sound or feeling which will bring back that positive state of mind.

TASK 2.6

Think of a time when you were very confident and were at your best. Turn the sound up, remember what you saw and what you felt. At the peak of the memory, touch your thumb and forefinger together. Do the same thing five times. What do you notice?

Work on yourself and be careful about the messages you give yourself. You may have spent years being "modest", thinking this was the right way to behave. However, confidence is an essential part of your enterprise package.

People will respond well to confidence but not to arrogance – you can still treat people with consideration and yet be quietly confident.

You need gradually to do more things and be relaxed about the outcome. If you are prepared to take action, relax and learn from your experiences. You have every right to be confident. Confidence should be based on the ability to have a go, rather than on being someone who never makes mistakes. The attitude you want is, "Whatever happens, I can turn this around" or "I can make this happen". Other people are attracted to confidence and are more likely to support you. Be the best and the most confident you can be. Remember you are only using a small part of your talents / capabilities / brain. Are you interested? Are you prepared to learn? If the answer to these two questions is "Yes", then be confident.

TIME MANAGEMENT

In being enterprising, you will have to challenge any of your habits that reduce your personal effectiveness. Your ability to make use of your time is crucial. A friend sent me a visual representation of the fact that you only have 86,400 seconds in a day and that it is the one resource which is going down every day. In that time, you want to be successful in your career / business and lead a happy and fulfilling life. However, there really only seems to be enough time to focus on one or the other. Nonetheless, you have to work with this valuable resource and get yourself the best deal.

Pareto's law applies clearly here: 20% of your time will produce 80% of the results. So, what are the key priority tasks that you need to focus on? Sometimes, these can be the most difficult tasks, but if you could deal with these personally, you might be able to delegate the other 80% of your tasks. You need to balance your time between things that are urgent now and things that are important. This is difficult, and something that those of you who have your own business will struggle with. There are always so many loose ends to tie up and decisions needed to keep the momentum of a project going. However, the strategic use of part of your time can mean less time needed to firefight in the long run.

The "power of now" is a good philosophy to have in the use of time. If you are at work, focus only on that the whole time you are at work. Do not take long lunch breaks or socialise too much. At the same time, when you are with your family or in recreational time, do not let work or other things intrude. That is what high performers in business do if they are also people who enjoy a happy family and personal life. I know we do advocate working on things you love, but some people use this as an excuse to make work everything, to always be at the office and never really leave it mentally when they come home. If Richard Branson and Alan Sugar always take weekends off, surely you can do the same.

Ability to say "No"
Linked to your ability to assert yourself, you should learn to say "No" to activities that you are not good at or which intrude on your time.

Managing several tasks
If you are involved in several projects, as I am usually, it can be difficult to know where to start and where to finish. The key again is to set time aside for each task and focus on it. There always has to be a degree of flexibility as unexpected things come up.

Time management systems

You need some type of time management system, whether manual or computerised. Plan your time ahead with a degree of flexibility. Again, you want to use the power of leverage to achieve results through the use of other people's time. If all you do is sell your time, as most professionals do, there is a limit to what you can achieve financially or otherwise.

Chunking

In project planning, it is a good idea to set a timetable and chunk down things into individual bits. As one commentator said, "How do you eat an elephant? Answer: One piece at a time".

At the start of each day, you need to ask yourself, "What can I do today to move my life forward?" and, at the end of each day, you need to ask yourself, "What did I do today? What contributions did I make?".

There can be a tendency among entrepreneurs to rule out community activities, thinking there will be plenty of time later for that when you retire. However, you do not know how long you have got. So, making a contribution, without looking for a return, can add immeasurably to your life and give you a perspective on things. I was particularly taken by a social enterprise set up in my own area by a church. They have created a modern trendy café with all profits going to third world enterprises and with an ongoing commitment to running community activities at the café as part of the ethos of the enterprise.

Momentum

Time taken to relax (remember your 15 minutes every day) is always time well spent. It will improve your creativity and reduce stress levels. Spending time relaxing and taking exercise are very strategic, as bad health can undermine all your activity. No matter how efficient, you are there is always room for improvement.

As well as your "timeouts", it is important to live every day as if it should not be wasted. How you would use your time if you were told that, if you were able to clear your work up over the next few days, a helicopter would be coming to take you to Acapulco for a free holiday. Would it concentrate your mind? Sadly, many of us only tend to work that way near urgent deadlines. We enjoy the adrenalin rush but the sad thing is normally we are wasting a lot of our time.

TASK 2.7

Keep a time log for a week, work out where you spend your time. Is there anything you would like to change? How much time are you spending on strategic long-term activities?

Time moves on and you can't go back. Make sure you are spending time on what is important for you. Although my aim is to show you how to be more enterprising, it should not be at the expense of the rest of your life.

I believe that an enterprising person values time and makes the best use of it. You have heard the old adage, "give a busy man something to do". Some people get through so much in a day in all aspects of their life; others never seem to have time for anything. Time is a resource, possibly the ultimate resource. You need to value it in all aspects of your life. Don't follow my example of paying £150 for a time management course, which I didn't have time to attend!

There are no magical systems but find one that works for you – surely one of your aims is to make the best use of your time now so that your business and family will both benefit in the long run. I see examples of people who have got the time equation wrong – successful business men in their 70s who are still working 60 hours a week or bored pensioners who retire early and, without the value of work, fill their time by watching soaps on the TV.

There is a tendency to live each day the same and to think that you have as much time as possible. Having lost a very close relative recently, who I rarely got to see because I was too busy, I wish I could go back and change how I spent that time. However, as Omar Khayyam, the ancient Persian poet, said, "The moving finger, having writ, moves on. Nor all their piety nor all thy wit shall change a single word of it". Food for thought.

TASK 2.8

What two things could you change now to make better use of your time?

HEALTH

I am the last person on earth to be lecturing anyone on health. But I know that most high performers have a lot of energy to achieve what they do because they watch their health.

You need to watch diet and to take exercise – 15 minutes of exercise, four times a week, a diet relatively low in carbohydrate and fat and your ongoing relaxation will all help with stress. There is an optimal level where you can enjoy stress but, beyond a certain point, it can cause difficulties. High blood pressure is something to monitor and regular health checks are also important. There is a tendency only to think about health when suddenly we don't feel well but, again, proactivity pays off.

For those of you at the early stage of your career, it may be hard for you to take health habits too seriously. However, although the wrong habits do not affect you now, those habits will be difficult to shift later on.

Strategic

Try and look both long-term and short-term on anything you are working on. A friend of mine was saying the other day that she had noticed in middle age that the people who had knuckled down to get qualifications or experience early on were reaping the dividends in career terms now. Is there anything you can spend time on now that will help you in the long run?

PERSONAL DEVELOPMENT

The focus of this chapter is on helping you to develop your potential and on challenging the "enemy within".

Unfortunately, we all have aspects of our personality that we would like to change. There are a lot of people who think personal development is "bunkum" and want to ignore it. There are others who attend every personal development course available and tend to build their favourite authors / speakers into guru status. However, they do not do anything to change themselves but keep spending more and more on the gurus' courses, convinced they will eventually get the secret.

There are many factors that have made us the people we are. To have any hope of change, first you must want to change. Second, you must accept that you will not change overnight but, instead, that you are on a journey and that, at times, it will seem very like one step forward and one step back.

This is particularly frustrating if you learn what to change and how to change it, and want to share your knowledge with others, but never get round to doing making the changes in yourself. The most effective teaching is not delivering a lecture but being a model for someone else because you have integrity and do what you say you are going to do.

The key to personal mastery is the ability to be self-aware and to seek feedback from people you trust. The annoying thing (tell me about it) is that it is much easier to help other people to change than to do it yourself. Accept that you are human and that, although you will not always talk your talk, you will do your best.

There is no one system that works for everyone. You will come across people who will advocate positive thinking, therapy or the works of one particular guru. However, there are no set answers, although basically all the models teach the same basic principles: relax, visualise, build your self-esteem, learn to control your emotions and take action. There is no set length of time this process will take. However, do put your personal development plan into practice.

TASK 2.9

What aspect of your behaviour would you like to change now? Work on it over the next 30 days.

Some changes will be easier than others, but even small changes make a big difference. The premise of this book is that you are only as strong as your weakest area. Work on it, improve it a little and you will leverage the effect on your life as a whole.

Find your own way to be the best you can be. It is also important that, whatever your career success, you be yourself. Be authentic. Be in control of your development and know not only where you want to end up but what type of person you can be. Success can be just as much of a challenge as failure. Are you still your same old self? As you develop your E-Factor skills and move forward, even though you are now a multimillionaire, a success in conventional terms, don't change. Underneath, you are still the same person who respects other people and will never sell out to the establishment.

Develop and remain the same. Quite a challenge.

3
NEGOTIATING THE DEAL

I believe your ability to assert yourself and negotiate to be one of the core competencies of enterprise. I do, however, have a confession to make, as like everyone, some of my E-Factor scores are better than others.

I have been proactive and been good at goal achievement and have even been accused of being "pushy" in the past. However, I am not naturally very good at dealing with aggression as I hate confrontation and will not always speak up as I should. I also am not very good at saying "No". These are all areas that I have had to work on. The whole point of the E-Factor analysis is to help you to work on all the areas, but particularly on any weakness that could block your progress. I have found to my cost, several times, in business that "niceness" can be perceived as weakness.

Assertion is, therefore, one of the 20% of activities that will make 80% of difference in my achievement. In other areas, such as finance or creativity, I have developed the necessary skills but assertion is an area where, once I develop the skills through practice, I may be able to help other non-assertive people better in the future, as I will know where they are coming from.

ASSERTION

Assertion is standing up for your rights, without hurting anyone else. Aggression, on the other hand, is where you are prepared to "walk over the top" of someone else to get what you want. Timidity, at the other extreme, is where you do not stand up for your rights and let others do whatever they want. Assertion is the middle ground.

People often confuse aggression with assertion. You will find a lot of aggressive people in business and, therefore, the myth is perpetuated that this is the way you must be in order to succeed in business. And so, even if they don't feel natural to do so, people try to follow this model.

However, if you do not consider the rights of other people and are overly aggressive, you may be met with opposition straight away, at which you might lose, or, even if you win a victory, there will be a cost – perhaps you will never be able to do business with that person or organisation again.

The ideal model has got to be "win-win", where you try, if possible, to create a deal where both sides get something.

But, let's be honest, it is sometimes better to be aggressive than to be too nice and to let other people always have the upper hand. It is an unfortunate aspect of human nature that people will take advantage of this niceness.

Why are we assertive / aggressive?

Your style of communication, be it assertive or aggressive, will vary with the different groups you communicate with and the different situations you find yourself in. For instance, a manager who is aggressive at work may be unassertive at home with his children, as guilt at working too much forces him to overindulge their every whim, while the teacher who may have no problem asserting themselves at school may be unable to assert themselves with his / her mother-in-law.

Again, our programming and our environment has played a part in shaping us. Parents want their children to be obedient and to do what they are told; schools want pupils to follow the rules. This can lead the model child to become a "yes man" as an adult and to have difficulty with authority figures. At the same time, aggression is increasing in our culture. The problem with being too nice is that avoiding conflict and keeping the peace can lead to resentment and potential aggression in the long run. You need to learn to say "No". For some, it is all they can say but politeness can go hand-in-hand with always saying "Yes". However, you must learn to stand up for yourself and get what you want. That is what negotiation is about.

Life consists of a series of deals with family, friends and business contacts. If you constantly take less than 5% of every deal, you do not get what you deserve and are driven by the fear of consequences. The danger is this can become a serious liability. I hope my suggestions will give you a framework to practise the middle ground behaviour.

When you are a child, your parents, or even big brothers / sisters, are there to stick up for you. When you are an adult, you have to adopt this role yourself. What you earn, how your life and business runs depends to a certain extent on your assertion skills. It is also a part of a good direct method of communicating with others. Other people will tread on your toes and try to take advantage sometimes without fully intending to. If you do not let them know directly, you are creating difficulties further down the line. Sometimes, non-assertive people will still want their way and will try to do it indirectly. They will manipulate and cajole and can be seen as devious, because they are not upfront with their feelings / thoughts. People feel comfortable dealing with someone with whom they know where they stand. If they make a deal, whatever the terms, they like to think that both parties will stick to it. Obviously, although honest communication is desirable, some form of subtlety is required.

TASK 3.1

Here is an assertion checklist. Please tick the areas you have problems with.

Tick ✓ to agree

1   I can never say "No".

2   I hate confrontation.

3   I am too aggressive.

4   I want to be liked.

5   I hate rejection.

6   I don't like speaking up.

7   I will put up with a lot.

8   I put myself down.

9   I find it difficult to cope with other people's aggression.

10 I don't like to make a fuss.

If you have ticked three or fewer of the areas, you have work to do. If you have ticked all of them, you will need to develop an assertion plan. If you have ticked none of them, congratulations. If you are not sure of the appropriate response to any of the areas, get feedback from others you can trust. People with assertion problems either believe they can't stand up for themselves at all or are blissfully unaware they have a problem, and take pride in their aggression.

The best communicator is the most flexible. If you want to build rapport with the other side in a negotiation, sometimes a more laid-back but firm style will work, sometimes you need to show the same level of assertion but adopt a strong approach. Again, assertiveness is a learned skill. Everyone needs to learn to be independent and to be proactive in seeking their own rights.

Everyday life

The beauty of assertion is that you can practise it in everyday life. Maybe you want to build up to asking your boss for a raise or to dealing with a difficult workmate, so you can start off with much simpler tasks, sending food back in a restaurant or saying "No" to someone who is trying to sell something in the street. I think I have got too good at this particular skill, since no-one selling something in the street ever seems to approach me!

Small victories and defeats matter. Record them and learn what you did wrong. I keep a journal and, every day, I record my victories and defeats.

Rehearsal

Suppose, for instance, that you have an interview, presentation or a difficult meeting coming up. It can be useful to role play in advance with a friend or colleague. Do this a couple of times and you will be better in the real situation. There's an old maxim, "The more you sweat in practice; the less you bleed in battle".

In putting your point across, it is important that you are congruent. You may not realise this but words only convey 5% of the meaning you are trying to communicate. The other 95% will be conveyed by tonality and body language. You may manage to say "No" but the full communication must show that you mean business, that you mean what you say. Again, you should have practice getting this "congruency" across. If you carry out role plays and rehearsals, this will help. There is nothing, however, to beat a real-life situation. It may only be telling your friends that you can't put them up on Saturday night, but it is a start. What is important is that doing the practice will eventually lead to you being yourself and saying what you feel no matter who you are dealing with.

Some of you may have great assertion skills in many areas but fail miserably in one or two other areas, which create real problems for you. Practise in the areas of situations in which you are weak.

And, although assertiveness is quite often taught in women's personal development courses, it is a problem for both men and women – it is NOT just a women's issue!

TASK 3.2

Identify the situations / types of people where / with whom you have difficulty being assertive. Which are the most critical? Pick one where you can work towards improvement.

Are you wrong being too nice?

Being agreeable, helpful or considerate to other people will go a long way. For those of you who are too aggressive and wonder why you get people's backs up, you can learn a lot by being nice from time to time.

However, it is not always appropriate to be nice. In particular, you need to identify situations when you would prefer to act differently and also know that you need to act differently but can't. What type of situations can this include? For instance, if someone is trying to "walk over the top of you" or insult you or your work, there is a need to be direct. If you feel powerless in this type of situation, that is definitely a liability. Also you need to realise that, if you are always too nice, people get fed up with your indecision. Someone who would regularly ask my opinion on their work performance got a little fed up recently when I gave my usual "nice" response, and said "You never give an honest opinion"!

Should everyone like you?

It is unlikely that everyone will like you – no matter how nice you are. Some people will dislike you without even knowing you and this can be a shock for us "people players". I remember, as a graduate entrant in National Westminster Bank, being put into a local branch to "learn the trade" and being hated for being a graduate on an accelerated scheme and for being Irish. The only answer was to be relaxed, to focus on work performance and to accept that, in time, people would take the time to get to know the "real me" (this approach did work!).

Your boss has given you a report to finish. You are really struggling and will not meet the deadline. Should you talk to her?

A passive person is likely to think of the worst consequences and be scared of what is going to happen. You must decide for yourself in your own life and come up with your own rules, shoulds and musts. You should talk to your boss, but not before **you** have decided what outcome you want for the meeting.

Telling the people

Many people who feel anger want to confront the person who has caused it, but instead they talk to third parties. Why? Sometimes, they can be scared of triggering off the other person's anger. It can be shocking to realise that other people do not have the same map of the world as you; they don't worry about offending people before they say what they think. People do not have to conform to your expectations and way of behaviour. The only person's behaviour you can change is your own. It is important that you act as you feel, and are not on the outside this person with no opinions and who is always nice but inwardly seething about everything. It is bad for your health, and self-esteem.

Why am I that way?

You were certainly not born too passive. Babies are naturally assertive to get their needs met. It is likely that it came from your environment, particularly from your family. My mother, God rest her soul, was a very good and kind individual. Like all parents, there is no training that goes with the job – we do the best we can. My father was very bad-tempered and, although he was different with at least one of my sisters, he did not accept answering back. The first time I answered my father back, I was 20. As a result, when people in authority or aggressive people try to bulldoze me into doing things I shouldn't do, my natural inclination is to say "Yes" to please them. This is an example of 20 years of programming. New behaviour has to be practised to get a different result – and I'm trying still.

Fear of consequences

Fear of consequences is an important inhibitor of assertiveness. Your imagination can run riot. You think, "If I tell this customer I can't do this work, they will get angry, they will go elsewhere". It is true that sometimes people will react as you anticipate. The problem is that you imagine it is going to happen every time – sometimes, the customers for whom you can't do the work immediately will be happy with a later deadline.

The fight or flight syndrome

These are two primitive responses which are in us all. Fight is the primitive response where you get ready to defend yourself. Flight is where you walk away from a situation where there could be a confrontation. Doing either all the time, as your only response to difficult situations is wrong but you need to choose carefully when to fight and when it's best to walk away.

Sometimes it can be good to get the clear head that comes from walking away, and sometimes by walking away you are simply making things worse. Only you can make that judgement as to which is the appropriate response.

It is difficult to control these feelings. What you have to deal with is what happens next. Change the focus of your response from your feelings to your next actions. Ask yourself a focusing question, "How can I take action here?".

Anger

We all feel anger at some time or other. Do you explode or implode? Neither is particularly good and yet anger is a natural emotion.

The problem is if you are nice when you should not be, you are going to be put upon. If this goes on too long, you will go straight from "nice" to "nasty temper". The problem with this is that you could create a mess. If your behaviour is like going up and down the gears of a car, one minute in first gear and then in fifth but never in the gears in between, you can expect an uncomfortable ride. You should be able to change your gear to suit the road life conditions; equally, you should be able to change your behaviour to suit the type of person and situation you face. If your child is in physical danger, that is not the time for passive Mr Nice. But you don't have to come over all aggressive when you're buying an icecream either.

People are not deliberately trying to hurt you when they ask for something to be done but, in getting something done, people naturally will look for the most accommodating provider, the one that meets their needs most closely. Start to be aware if you are giving off too strong a signal, saying "Choose me". It only makes sense to be chosen when your needs meet the customer's needs. Look to make small changes in your behaviour that give you a better chance of operating effectively.

It's all a game

To change your behaviour to improve any of the E-Factors you need to practise. The first time you use any of the strategies, it will probably not work. However enjoy it, it is a game you are playing.

What is difficult about behaviour like assertion is that, once you start to use some of the strategies, you will come up against resistance on all sides. Your friends and family who are used to taking advantage of you won't like the "new you". Persevere – and ease it in slowly, so that one day they realise that you have changed but they haven't noticed the steps along the way.

Watch your language
The words you use to communicate can be unfortunate. Don't over apologise. It's little phrases like, "I'm so sorry to ask you this", that dilute the message you are trying to communicate. Start to observe both the internal chat in your head and how you speak to others – and change it.

Stop!
Every time, you tell yourself off, say to yourself "Stop!". Ask yourself the question, "How can I prove myself here?"

TASK 3.5

Next time you catch yourself apologising for nothing or using passive language, say "Stop!"

Strategies
Certain things are important when you are being assertive – for example, maintaining eye contact, not smiling, not getting drawn into a conversation and keeping the conversation as short as possible.

The status quo

In work or within a business, there always seems to be a pecking order. People tend to treat other people according to their status, even if no formal organisation exists. The ironic thing is that, every day, you will alter your behaviour depending on who you are with. Quite often, you will vary your body language, tonality and words.

Where appropriate, you have to act to raise your status.

Someone with **high** status:

1   Takes their time.

2   Uses silence.

3   Listens without comment.

4   Maintains eye contact.

You can also lower your status, for effect. Let us say you have a friend who earns less than you and has got used to you helping them out, manipulating constantly to get their own way. Play them at their own game: lower your status, use sympathy, show you support their position and wish you could help if only you can afford it. Always remember you have a choice to play, either as a 10 (high status) or as a 1 (low status), or somewhere in between.

It is important to sometimes change your status level to be assertive in the appropriate way. No doubt, you will get it wrong a few times but you will learn quickly.

Practice

Deliberately have nice days when you are all sweetness and light and some (only a few, please!) not-so-nice days where you are more direct and forthright.

Look for any opportunity, no matter how small, to practise these assertiveness skills. There is no need to change your personality, or who you are, altogether. Remain "nice" but be someone nice with an edge, who can adapt to circumstances and different people and communicate properly.

I cannot emphasise enough how the use of some of these techniques can change your enterprise performance by itself. People trying to encourage enterprise spend a lot of money giving promoters help on business fundamentals and on completing their business plans. However, this help will go to waste if the budding entrepreneur is unable to be assertive. Let me show you the areas where a lack of assertion can count against the enterprising person.

1   Being given a poor deal by their bank manager.

2   Being bullied by suppliers and customers.

3   Customers taking too long to pay.

4   Paying too much for everything.

5   Conflict with partners.

6   Breaching ethical rules to please customers.

7   Being bullied by government agencies.

The list goes on. In business, you will come across aggressive business people who will try to win at any cost, government agencies that will bully you, difficult customers, suppliers and staff who will try to impose their rules on you. You will need to stand up for your business and yourself or you will not survive. I have found assertiveness to be a core business and life skill, and yet again something which is not taught through the academic curriculum.

NEGOTIATION

Negotiation is a process and has some similarity to sales, which is covered in the chapter on personal influence (**Chapter 6**). Sales is really just one type of negotiation, as you make deals in almost every aspect of your business. In doing any deal, you need to assert your rights, otherwise you will get a poor deal, lose money or lose ground.

"Everything is Negotiable"
Gavin Kennedy, an Edinburgh professor, wrote a book with this title. It is a good mindset. We can all believe in fixed procedures, set rules or set prices, but they should be challenged.

There are no set prices. Some of us naturally love to haggle; for others, it is an embarrassment. However, if you don't ask, you don't get. It all depends on the deal. Suppliers may be prepared to reduce the price of product if there are other certainties / favourable points built into the deal for them.

"The Art of the Deal"
This is the name of a book written by Donald Trump, who spends most of his life putting together property deals. He makes the point that deal-making is more of an art than a science. You need to learn to find your own style that works for you. The traditional negotiation model is of "playing aggressive hardball". However, that may not be suitable in the circumstances or may not be your style.

Your own negotiation style

Your negotiation style will be unique to you – but there are some threads to consider.

Do your homework
As with sales, you need to prepare before the deal. You need your technical data and you need to know the personalities of the other people involved in the deal and what are their key objectives.

You will also learn a lot face-to-face during the negotiation. You will sense how much the other party wants to deal and, on that basis, you may need to adjust your own strategy.

The deals you make are the life you make
Your career / enterprise is very dependent on your deal-making capabilities. Your relationships are also a deal, and you have got to strike a fair compromise.

It is very easy to get the deal wrong. If a key condition or pricing structure is left out, the whole deal can fail.

Decide what you want
You need to know what outcomes are essential for you to get in the deal, and what outcomes are merely desirable. This will help you decide what you can afford to trade to get the outcomes you really want, as you may be required to trade something in the course of the deal.

Rapport and understanding
It is important to build some sort of rapport with the other party (or parties to the deal). You need to spend time getting to know each other and your respective positions. You are unlikely to agree with the other side's perspective, but it is useful to seek to understand it and to try, if possible, to create a "win-win" situation, where they get what they want, while you also get what you want. If you try to get everything, to win every point, you may create a bad relationship, leading to no further deals, as well as a reputation as someone who has to take everything in a deal. There is strategic value in giving the other side something.

Decide where to start and where to end
If you start off by stating exactly what you want, you will end up getting less. People will usually pitch lower until they see the position.

Be prepared to walk away
It will always be to your advantage if you are genuinely prepared to walk away when the deal is not right. The other party will remember this and it will strengthen your position in future negotiations.

Get the deal in writing
A lot of older business people like to think when they have shaken hands on a deal that the transaction is sacrosanct – but you always need a written signed contract to spell things out, in the event of any future dispute.

Don't take things personally
Things may be said during a negotiation that sometimes could lead to offence being taken. A negotiation is no time to be too sensitive. Your ability to remain relaxed, but focused on the outcome, is critical.

Creativity
A negotiation is not a time to stick to one position only. You may have fall-back positions but your challenge sometimes is to find a lateral "win-win" outcome, particularly where there is deadlock.

Who has the leverage?
Who has the strongest position? If it is you, make sure you use whatever leverage you have. If the other party has it, giving up is not the best option. Even when they are in a weak position, good negotiators sometimes can make the positions seem more balanced, simply by the way they use their leverage.

I remember a small business client, who had run up an unapproved overdraft of £30,000 and, therefore, was in serious trouble with her bank, berating her bank manager for not looking after her properly, totally wrongfooting him and changing the balance in the negotiating situation.

Review their perceptual position
People do see things differently. Your ability to see things from other people's perceptual position is an important skill in negotiating.

TASK 3.6

Take time out. Think of a situation where you are at loggerheads with someone else. Imagine you are the other person. What are you thinking? What do you (as the other person) want out of the negotiation?

Then change roles and become a third party, not involved in the deal. How do you see the situation from this new position?. Can you identify what both parties want? How can you help them to a "win-win" outcome?

Now return to your own role – what have you learnt that will help you in your negotiation?

Opening offers

Your opening offer is crucial. If you are too near to what you really want, you will end up nowhere near it as, in many cases, your offer will be seen as merely an opening gambit and the other party will hope to get a much better deal. It may be better to make a tough opening offer, provided it is still credible. You need to convince the seller that you still want genuinely to buy their product. It is also a good idea if you can convince the seller you do not have the funds to meet their opening offer.

You do need to be tough and refuse to be intimidated. You should never give concessions without getting something back. What you are trying to get across is a psychological message: "if you want something, it is going to cost you".

Do not accept their first offer

This is the worst thing you can do in a negotiation. Not only is the first offer likely to be their "worst offer" but because the other party will expect you to haggle, by accepting someone's first offer you will make them worried that they have got it wrong and so they may begin to look to negotiate you down even further!

I can't emphasise enough that, once the first offer is made, is when the dealing is done. For instance, at one stage of my career, I got a job I really wanted and needed. I wasn't particularly happy with the salary offered but I accepted it immediately, thinking that I could easily increase my salary package once I was in the organisation. I found to my dismay that this was not how it worked. The time to sort out the deal was now over – and I never got the salary I wanted, although I know now that I might have got it had I negotiated harder at the right time.

Look for tradeoffs

If you have a grievance, focus on getting something more from the deal.

What if?

This is your key question to ask when making the deal. It is too late to ask afterwards. You have to get answers to all sorts of contingencies and change the deal to reflect them, as necessary.

Learn to enjoy it

Research I have carried out on top negotiators show that they love to deal. It may not come naturally to you and you may find it embarrassing initially but, rest assured that if you don't or won't negotiate, you will get much less out of life financially and otherwise. You need to learn to enjoy negotiating. Negotiation is a game and you can get better simply by playing the game.

Let us say you are getting a new cleaner for your house. Practice deal-making, make sure you get a fair deal. Work up to where you could negotiate with your bank manager or boss at work.

Reputation

Work on your business reputation. Deals will be much easier for you if you have the right reputation. "Hard but fair" is the type of reputation you want. The reputation of "very easy to deal with" can leave you with a reputation as a pushover. Equally, if you constantly make deals and then don't stick to them, this will run your credibility in negotiations.

How do you get a reputation as a good negotiator? Two ways:

1   How you have handled previous negotiations.

2   PR.

Later in the book, we look at your personal marketing (**Chapter 4**). It is important to think through how you present yourself, as that is often how you are perceived by other people.

The details

The details do matter – in fact, often the deal is in the details. This can include everything from what you wear to where the venue is. If details emerge that change the structure of the deal, be prepared to use the changes to your advantage.

In an ideal world, every deal should be run through a piece of software that could pick up the potential for miscommunication and conflict – sadly, such software does not yet exist. So using "what if" questions can be useful to ensure clarification – even a minor point that is overlooked can be crucial later on.

TASK 3.7

Go out and search for a consumer item such as a new TV. It is preferable if the item is something you want to buy, since there is no practice like the real thing, but, if not, use the situation as an opportunity to negotiate a deal. Unless you actually want to buy the item at the end of the negotiation, end by saying that you will go away and think about the purchase. Practise your negotiating skills. What did you learn?

Review

What you need to overcome is the embarrassment of asking for a reduction in price or a change in a deal, particularly when the other side is likely to make you believe that the terms are fixed. When you make someone a really low offer for something with a high mark-up, they will be shocked and, initially, possibly angry. You hear people using the phrase, "I won't insult you with a silly offer" – usually just before they do – but good business people are not afraid to make low offers, particularly if they are used to buying and selling. They believe that you can make an offer as low as you like, and sell as high as you like. One author recommends you go into an electrical goods shop where you see a TV priced, say, for £500. Walk up to the salesman and offer him £30, just to get used to the reaction.

I am not recommending that you always aim to take advantage of people, but you must get used to the fact that, in many cases, other people will value their products, services and assets much greater than you do. Unless your aim is to get people to like you, to pay over the odds constantly and to lose money, you are going to have to learn to negotiate.

There may be occasions when you bring someone in to negotiate on your behalf, but it is not practical to do so all the time. As life is a series of deals, the ability to negotiate is highly valued.

Posture

In negotiating situations, it is important that you get your posture right. Opponents are looking for signs of weakness, or over-eagerness to agree. Equally, if you appear too arrogant or aggressive, there is a danger of alienating the negotiator or their advisor.

The element of surprise can be useful, particularly where the other negotiators are overplaying the status card. For example, Inland Revenue investigators expect businesspeople to be on the defensive, since all the cards are stacked in the favour of the investigators, who have strong powers and adopt a very threatening posture. They also expect that accountants usually will be compliant, because a lot of their work depends on their relationship with the Inland Revenue, so they will tend not to be too assertive. This is not really fair representation for the businessperson. So, one businessman took an innovative approach to these negotiations – he brought a top QC to the meeting. Although the QC was not even a tax barrister, he turned the table on the investigators, asking them a string of questions and forcing them to adopt a different approach. I am not criticising the Inland Revenue, simply showing this as an example of how parties will often act a certain way if they have status control. The ironic thing is that good negotiators are like poker players and you would never guess that, on paper, they are at a severe disadvantage on negotiations.

I do sympathise (well, maybe only for a moment) with possible bargaining positions you find yourself in. For example, suppose you are applying for your first job after university, you desperately want to get into publishing and this is the only offer you have received; or you have started a small business organising events, you have got no business in your first three months and now a local council has asked you to organise its Halloween firework display. Your natural response is "where do I bite their hand off"?

However, negotiating has two agendas. The other party doesn't want to overpay, although they do expect any prospective supplier worth their salt to negotiate. If the supplier doesn't negotiate, they worry whether they will be able to carry out the project the way it should be done.

If you get the deal on the wrong terms, you will find it hard to increase your salary or your price for future council projects. Yes, there may be some deals or opportunities lost because you stuck to your guns but there's much greater potential that when you get deals, you will get the right one.

Remember too that you cannot do every deal. I am reminded of an old John West Salmon advertisement, "It is the fish that John West reject that makes John West the best". Some of the best deal-making you ever do will be the deals you walk away from.

For instance, not so long ago, everyone was into buy-to-let property and, as a result, there were significant rises in house prices and it was difficult to get rental returns to cover mortgage interest and expenses. But good businesspeople were prepared to sift through a lot of bad deals to find the ones that were self-funding. If you can make property deals that self-fund, you can do more property deals. But if you must pay part of the mortgage yourself and want to do more similar deals, hoping for long-term appreciation, your cash flow is potentially catastrophic. Your deal-making skills really come into play here.

Keep your options open

It is always good to have other options in a deal, other than feeling under threat to complete the deal as proposed by the other party. If you are trying to increase the price your major customer pays, you need to have sought out alternatives and, if necessary, to be prepared to walk away if they refuse to budge. I always find it amazing how attractive an employee can become to an employer, when other people are offering them better packages to go and work for them. Again, perception is important, and, like much of your achievement, a lot will depend not on the actual reality but how you value yourself, because that is likely to be how others will value you as well. In an ideal world people will give you as much as you deserve, but that is not how it works in practice. If you want anything, you have to ask for it.

I think we should end this section by looking at a short case study relating to negotiation and assertion to illustrate they are core competencies you must develop. You may not be a capitalist but, if you want to make things happen, you will need to work with other people, gather resources and implement. All these stages require negotiation skills. Are you working on yours?

Case study

Jean has been taken on as a graduate trainee by a local charity. They want her to run a new project to raise £250,000 a year for the charity and to build up the volunteer base and corporate sponsorship. What situations and issues will Jean face where she may need her negotiation skills? Please spend at least 10 minutes on your answer before turning to **Appendix 1** for my thoughts on Jean's situation.

Observation

As well as practising some of the ideas contained here, I recommend you start observing people and any dealing / bartering situation you find yourself in. If you find something useful, try to apply it straight away. Keep a mini record of your new negotiation life. Review every deal you make, no matter how small. What can you learn from these deals?

Perhaps you can also do deals on behalf of others. The ironic thing is that, because you are a third party and not emotionally involved in the deal, you probably will do better deals for them than you do for yourself.

At times, I have advocated a fairly hardnosed approach to negotiation. However, I am still not a fan of taking 100% and leaving the other party nothing. They are less likely to stick to the deal and, at the very best, will tend to badmouth you. Try to be strategic; don't shoot yourself in the foot in the long run. Try always to be honourable, although that does not mean saying "Yes" to deals that don't suit you or are unfair.

Every deal is different, will progress at different rates and will have its own subtle nuances. You need to apply the basic success principle: Know what you want before you start, do the negotiations, decide where to make the pitch and be flexible. Try to change what you can offer if the other side has particular needs and you are still getting what you want. Flexibility is the key to success deals – and that includes flexibility in getting out.

Develop negotiation skills and, I promise you, you will be welcome in any industry. In an ideal world, the meek should prosper, but always remember "blessed is the dealmaker"!

Conclusion

Hopefully, you can see that, just because an area of work is not obviously a business venture, this does not preclude the need for negotiation. Some people seem to be born dealmakers. When I was 9, I used to buy a quarter of sweets, take them to church and, in the children's church, sell sweets for the children's collection. This happened for three weeks, until the helper put a stop to it. I enjoyed doing deals but, later, as I focused more and more on my schoolwork, I didn't really build my dealing skills. As someone who just wants the job done, it is easy to do poor deals just to move a project on. However, like many other people, I have had to realise that almost anything in life is dependent upon a deal. If the deal is right, everything will flow. Make a bad deal in business or personal life and, despite your best efforts, things will not work out.

4
PERSONAL BRANDING

Marketing is not just a function needed by large or small businesses. It is an attitude of mind in which your company or organisation sets out to meet the needs of a defined market and organises all its activities to meet them. To be successfully enterprising, you need to think of yourself as a company. Whether you are setting up a business or working for a company, you are a one-man / one-woman personal services company and you need to use the concepts of marketing to get yourself the best deal in the marketplace.

You need to do ongoing market research and develop your own marketing mix to achieve your goals. There was an interesting book published in America, where a marketing consultant applied marketing concepts to the mission of finding a suitable husband or wife. This is not my arena but its success as a bestseller illustrates a recognition that marketing techniques can be used in your career or business. It may also illustrate how desperate some people are to find a partner!

YOU ARE THE BRAND

Everyone knows about the Beckham brand. The couple are recognised as a worldwide brand because they have been marketed as such. Everything you do, wear or say adds to the perception other people have of you. You need to be clear what image / impression you want to give and to make sure you don't get involved in activities that conflict with the market you are aiming to reach.

I once came across a young lawyer who was aiming to build a practice with large established customers in a local town. The image he needed to project was that of someone business-like, a "safe pair of hands" respected in the local community. To his (not just financial) cost, he got involved in a "get rich quick" scheme, which involved getting other people to buy what turned out to be dodgy shares. Clients who came into his office to get advice about their legal structure found themselves being harangued to join the scheme. The young lawyer, as is often the case, didn't make any money out of the get rich quick scheme. More importantly, he destroyed his chances of being seen as the safe pair of hands any more. It was a big blow to his long-term prospects of gaining any kind of local market share.

What type of brand image do you want to project?
The only way to answer this question is to ask another question: "Who is your customer?". Let us say, for instance, that you want to appeal to one of the major consultancies, such as Accenture, so that they will recruit you as an employee. You need to find out early on what type of person they are looking for and what evidence would be useful in showing that you are that type of person. If you found out, for instance, that they wanted someone enterprising who could take responsibility for projects, you could look at your track record and consider becoming an intern for the student enterprise centre or look for some student activities where you could take responsibility for making an event or project happen. The difficulty with this strategy is that you must be sure that you are not trying to change your personality and activities just to get a job with a company for which you are not suited.

It seems that there's a conflict with the earlier advice to "be yourself". The point is that it is important to recognise what you are interested in and good at, and then to use marketing strategies to achieve what you want. You may not be the greatest talent the publishing industry has been looking for but, if the industry is not aware of you and you don't get yourself into a position to show that you can make a contribution, you have no chance. Many of you have been brought up to keep yourselves out of the limelight and not to put yourself forward. However, it is a very competitive world and you need to get a competitive advantage if you are to succeed.

Market research

If you are building a business, not only do you need to assess market need at the start of the business but also on an ongoing basis. Markets change and you may need to change the focus of your products or services to meet those changing requirements. The same applies to corporate or community careers. What are the key qualities needed? What does the market need?

Not only do you need to show market awareness of whatever industry you are in, you need to know what the employment and business market is looking for. For instance, many businesses and companies want their new graduates to be enterprising and innovative. How can you demonstrate these qualities and your capacity to act that way in the job situation? Are there courses being run in innovation? What type of work experience could you get in the holidays?

Market research information can be obtained both formally and informally. Read market reports on the trends in your industry of choice, find out what statistical data says about the size of the market for the industry's products or services. Informal information can also be useful – for example, knowing what is a key driver for a chief buyer in a major company or what are the major preferences of the recruitment team. I found informal information to be very useful prior to an interview for my first job in accountancy with a major industrial company. This was my one opportunity to get into an excellent training scheme. Informal information-gathering allowed me to find out that the main recruiter was focused on all student trainee accountants being committed to qualifying. It was very useful to know this – I was genuinely committed to qualifying but knowing his key preference helped in marketing my services.

Whatever your business ambitions, you need to have access to information. Building networks will help, as will awareness of published market research available. You must not ignore what the market tells you. That is the main principle of marketing, which separates it from selling.

What are your customers or potential customers saying? What needs do they have? What benefits do they want? Will they still be looking for the same things in the long term? Do their needs / benefits match with the product / service you offer? If not, what value can you add to your offering to make it more likely that you can do business with them? If you can't do business, you may need to look at the market again to find a different niche to pursue.

Note that this market research information is only of any use if you base your future activities on it. Never assume that, because you already are in business or have experience of an industry, that you know all the answers; you need to ask the market, respect its responses and adjust your marketing plan accordingly. You also must keep abreast of developments and respond appropriately. As a small business, if you do not respond to changes, your business is in trouble.

Your marketing should be more than just simply making a sale or getting that job. It should be strategic. If you are the product, where are you on the product cycle? Where will the market be in five years' time? Are you positioning yourself strategically to take advantage of future opportunities?

TASK 4.1

What market information do you need? How can you get it
at minimum financial or time cost to yourself?

SWOT analysis

This is a standard analysis that companies carry out on product offerings, looking at strengths, weaknesses, opportunities and threats. Still keeping on the theme that you are the product, in personal marketing, it is important to analyse where you are as regards the market, having already done your market research.

What are your strengths with regard to the opportunity offered? What are your weaknesses? What are the key opportunities that you could develop? What are the threats that challenge your business venture or career opportunity?

Let us say you have decided to set up a student enterprise networking club. What do you have to offer that will help develop the project? Do you have contacts who will help? Have you any marketing background or access to finance? What weaknesses do you have as a recent graduate? Is there something missing? Do you have the clout to make things happen? Have you experience of running a networking club before? Do you have the necessary management skills? Is there a clear opportunity for a networking club now? Is the opportunity local or is it nationwide? Is the opportunity a good profit model or should it be a social enterprise? What threats are there? Is there a similar established organisation that people can join, which would form your major competition? What specific risks, financial or otherwise, does the project have?

TASK 4.2

Do a SWOT analysis of yourself in relation to your business or career objectives. What does your SWOT analysis tell you?

Unique selling proposition

What is your USP or unique selling proposition? What do you offer that nobody else does? What is your competitive advantage? What separates you from any other competitors?

Product

What is your product? What are you actually offering? What service, product or information are you offering the market-place? What exactly will you do? What is your proposition in one sentence?

Price

Price is a key marketing component. How do you price yourself on the market? What are you worth? What market are you after? Where are you positioning yourself?

How have you worked out your price? Are you prepared to hold out for it? Are you a £50 per day, a £500 per day or a £2,000 day person? Your price will be affected by demand, to put it bluntly. If you want to be a trainee lawyer, there are loads of law graduates looking for places in legal firms, so the firms can keep salaries down.

Key questions when looking at your business product – you – are where do you see pricing going in the long run, and what is your strategy to get there?

Place

Lots of questions here: Where are you going to operate from? Where will you reach your clients? Will you make use of modern technology? How international is your product or service? What is your distribution system? How will people access you, either within the company or in the world? Have you the capacity to reach out to the emerging markets in India and China?

Promotion

It is important to have a good marketing mix. Your product, price and place must be in line with what the market has shown it needs. However, in marketing yourself, once you have identified who and where your customer is, you create your offering to suit the market. The key part of the marketing mix is to make your market aware that you are available and appropriate for marketing needs. In some cases, this may lead directly to sales but, in many cases, you and your key advisers may need to use personal influence to close the deals that good promotional activity will cause.

We are all a little bit uneasy as to how celebrities continually promote themselves or the lengths that those who fall off the ladder will go to get back up there. However, if you want to make that business work, get that job and continue to get opportunities, you need to first of all be comfortable with the concept of self-promotion. It would be nice if your good work was enough to ensure you got the results you required but, even in traditional professions today, there is a recognition that you need to make other people aware of what you do and to promote your brand.

Guerrilla marketing

It would be nice to have a huge marketing budget but, realistically, you will have to adopt the same strategy as many small businesses. You will have to be a "guerrilla marketer" – that is, you will have to adopt promotional strategies that produce maximum results with minimum expense. The key is maximum publicity and awareness.

Advertising

You need to always be wary of advertising, which has to be targeted and produce measurable results. In creating brand awareness, often you will get much greater impact by using more subtle methods, for instance, a newspaper column which could promote you as an expert.

Ideally, any form of promotion should be considered that could produce results. You should research and experiment to find out what works best. In the professions, there is a perception that a professional who has to advertise for work must not be any good. That's fine and dandy for established professionals, but how do you get work when you first put up your nameplate and don't have a list of customers?

You also need to promote not only to get business but to get the type of work you are looking for in the long run. Let us suppose that, long term, you want to work in an investment bank but, short term, you are prepared to accept any job in financial services. Where possible, promote yourself to a market segment that will have some type of link, however tenuous, with investment banking – for example, to a financial institution that has an investment banking arm – that should make a transfer to investment easier.

Whatever media you use in promoting yourself, you need to be clear about what you want to achieve. One graduate, who started out as an architect, had a simple strategy to get as much work as possible. He promoted himself everywhere effectively, getting lots of small jobs and a reputation as "the cheapest in town". However, two years later, he found himself with lots of small work at low margins and with no time to target the large building contractor market he was really aiming for. He had to sell that practice and completely "rebrand" himself.

Hopefully, it is also obvious that you need to use a media that will reach your target audience. It may please friends and family to see your article in your local paper on your stockbroking expertise in London. Much more effective would be something read by people in the profession or by people who are looking to invest significant sums with a stockbroker in your area.

AIDA

This should always be the underlying design model for any promotional activity you undertake. The letters stand for:

A Attention   Make the customer aware.
I Interest   Attract their interest.
D Deal   Get them to deal with you.
A Action   Get them to take some action (ideally, buy from you!).

TASK 4.3

You are a newly qualified chartered surveyor and want to promote your career in commercial property in London. What three things can you do to make it happen?

Public relations

Newspapers and magazines are always looking for interesting material. Newsworthy material will be published. Interesting articles will be read. And people do believe what they read in newspapers and magazines.

You need to look for opportunities to make the news. Effective PR is all about building a relationship, either directly with journalists or indirectly through a PR consultant.

As well as using the media, you can also give services or products "pro bono" to create awareness – this can be very effective. It is vital you are committed to the charitable cause, as celebrities have learnt to their cost that agreeing to work with a charity for profile and then cancelling engagements in favour of more commercial opportunities results in negative PR.

Remember, since you are a brand, although you may not be under media scrutiny like the Beckhams, everything you do counts. If you are promoting an image as someone who supports family values, living the life of a playboy shows you as a hypocrite – not good PR.

However, the person who is clever at personal marketing will try to use whatever their competitive advantage is and, indeed whatever situation they find themselves in, whatever the problem.

Networking and word-of-mouth marketing

You need to harness the power of positive word-of-mouth. Join networks that will help you meet people who are eminent in your field. You need to have a system to make contacts and also to keep in touch with them. A network almost has a financial worth. Some people in your network will know people who know people who will be able to explain or help with key areas that could prove of use to your business or career. Again, networking may not cost money directly, but you need to work for it. It requires effort, planning and organisation. If you go to a networking event, you should set goals, review your performance and have a systematic way of keeping in touch with new contacts.

The key thing in personal marketing is to use the power of word-of-mouth marketing. Networks are only one of a number of methods that could prove effective in getting the geometric progression available from word-of-mouth marketing. What else will get your profile out there? Consider workshops, seminars, blogs, the internet and other ways to deliver word-of-mouth marketing.

The key lesson is you can't sit and wait for positive word-of-mouth marketing to work. You must positively influence the process and make sure that you use the most powerful tools available to you.

Other promotional activities

You can also use free samples, point-of-sale displays, competitions or numerous other promotional techniques. Again, the techniques you use must be suitable for you.

For those of you who have a service, you don't quite have to go to the extent of the actor Jean-Claude Van Damme, who did high kicks outside a restaurant where a Hollywood producer always dined in order to attract the producer's attention. But, you get the idea. Find a way for a large company or customer to sample your services without any obligation.

The type of promotion you choose depends on:

- The stage of the product life cycle that has been reached (see below).
- The nature of the product itself.
- The size of your budget (if any).
- The nature of the target market.

Market segments

Which market segment or segments are you after? You can divide your potential customers according to various factors, including income, gender and region. You need to decide which segments you are after and why.

If you target all small businesses with less than five employees, you must be sure that this will meet your strategic purposes. Businesses of this size are unlikely to have a budget to fund growth consulting or a high paying job position. However, such businesses, because of their small size, often offer a greater opportunity to get real involvement that will give you real responsibility and the opportunity to make a difference.

TASK 4.4

Suppose you want to be a sales consultant for a pet products business. Divide up the possible market segments; decide which one to go after and why.

Market segmentation is important because your message needs to be targeted clearly at one or two groups. You are likely to be less focused (and thus less successful) if your market is "everyone". Ideally, as a business person, it is good to find a niche where your experience and resources will leverage high results.

Packaging

How do you package yourself and your work? Packaging can include how you dress and your personal appearance; it can also include how services are laid out, and how your portfolio will appear.

Product enhancement

You should be continuously trying to improve your knowledge, qualifications, and experience to enhance the "product", which, in this case, is you.

Branding

It is important that you develop a brand that people recognise and that you try to encourage customer loyalty.

Product life cycle

For your business or your career, you should analyse where it is in the product life cycle. For instance, if you are opening a sandwich bar, this is not a new concept unless you have some very innovative features. If you have decided to become a celebrity through the power of "reality TV", you should be very careful how you use this vehicle, since many of these programmes are now flagging. On the other hand, business programmes are still at an early stage of their lifecycle and, therefore, might be a better vehicle towards celebrity status.

You need to come up with new strategies or markets for products that are reaching saturation point, while you will need a very effective guerrilla marketing system if you are at an early stage and are looking at a pioneering role. For example, let us say you want to be England's first professional bullfighter. Since this idea is at an early stage in its product life cycle, you will need to adapt your marketing ideas appropriately.

Watch how other people market themselves

Watch someone who is building a professional reputation or someone who is building a celebrity profile. What steps do they take? Watch how they try to keep their profile up.

Celebs spend at least 25% of their time promoting their profile. You need to invest at least 10% of your time, no matter how busy you are at present, in marketing yourself and keeping your profile up. If you have one major customer or employer who is paying you very well, it is natural to think "Why bother?". However, if you fall out with that key source of income, suddenly you could be in difficulty without the income or career profile that will help your marketing activities. Remember the old truism from careers advisers, "It is easier to get a job when you have one".

I constantly see some students, who attend business events in their holidays to make contacts, enjoy their search for future opportunities. I see lots of others who can't be bothered and are "too busy" to explore these opportunities. Obviously, I hope you are different if you have taken the time and effort to read this book.

Cross-fertilisation

You can be enterprising if you apply business practices that work in one industry to another. For instance, if you have worked in the highly competitive world of financial services where marketing is a key element and you go to work for a firm of architects who do not know marketing, adapting one of the marketing strategies from financial services could be highly innovative and profitable for the architectural practice.

The benefit of varied approaches

Just like depending on one client, depending on one personal marketing strategy is not enough. I know one young accountant, who built his practice on presenting start-up seminars for small business start-ups for local enterprise agencies. Although he got lots of business, there were two problems with this approach: first, although he got lots of business, he was not getting established business – once the start-ups had started, he had no further dealings with them – and, second, when the enterprise agencies started to take the sessions themselves to save money, he had no alternative strategy.

Different activities can help each other, provided they are part of a co-ordinated plan. They open up your services to a wider variety of sources and each method of marketing will impact the other, hopefully positively.

YOUR PERSONAL BRAND

Remember that you are a brand and that everything counts. This includes not only your activities but also everything from your posture, voice, tonality and small talk – each can make a difference. Like me, you might get a shock if you were videoed to show how other people see you. We would all prefer not to watch these films but as you can imagine, if you can relax, you will learn a lot. It is very difficult otherwise to see and hear how we appear to others when presenting our personal brand.

Online

Something you have to accept is that, although "dot coms" are not necessarily always the favourite mode of business these days, you must make sure that your online profile matches up with your brand and the marketing message you want to present.

I learnt this lesson in an interesting way. My 10-year-old son, bored at school, decided to "Google" his father. Sounds like a painful process but, as the modern techno-kid that he is, he likes to use all available resources and gadgetry. When I was "Googled", that is, looked up, he found me at my place of work but found a very limited, almost non-existent, profile. Whose fault was this? None other than my own. If someone was considering doing business with me or an associated company, one of the first things they would do is to use the power of internet to check up on my profile.

Marketing practitioners reckon that, as part of your personal marketing agenda, you should be very careful with your marketing information. On the internet, as in everything you do in your use of it, your membership of online communities and participation all will play a part in your marketing efforts, certainly in the strategic sense as this becomes more and more important. As we have already discussed, word-of-mouth is very important and internet activity, handled properly, gives you the opportunity to reach out worldwide with your "blagging".

Branding is very much about the image that people have of you. It is sensible not to expect everyone to like you. However, if you want to achieve significant career or commercial success, you need to have more control of other people's perception of you. The key question to ask yourself is "Do the right people notice what I do?". If the answer is "No", you need to take corrective action. If you don't care, fine, but accept that the right people are those who will make the key commercial decisions. Yes, if you do good work, you deserve results but, sadly, that is not how it always works. Other people need to hear what you have done, too.

As part of your personal branding, try to be more interesting and focus on the activities that will get results. If there is a forum where you can let other people know what you have done – for instance, a company newsletter – let them know. They always will be searching for newsworthy items. If there is an opportunity to speak your mind, do so. As said elsewhere, you will always be communicating something (even if it's nothing), so make sure it is the message you want to convey.

Opportunity

To stand out, you or your company need to be different. You need to see things differently, that is why creativity and seeing different angles can be important. Many times, you have to work with both yourself and what you do now and use that to find a breakthrough to do different things. Being enterprising is all about open-mindedness and being prepared to take action to do something. Again, as suggested in the creativity chapter (**Chapter 1**), sometimes the new solution will come from looking at an industry or area that you have never considered before.

Again, you should be marketing yourself inside and outside work, making the best use of your time and effort. I think a range of activities is important but, sometimes, you will find a key opportunity that will provide an opportunity to maximise your profile.

Where are you now?
As you know, I recommend that you try to measure where you are now. It is like the example I gave where I noticed that I was not paying enough attention to my online profile. It could be a shock for you, too, to realise that your profile is not out there. Do something about it. Can you, in one or two sentences, explain exactly what you do for your employer or customer, what benefit you provide and what is your unique selling proposition? You must then get that message out, in whatever form your "guerrilla marketing" strategy takes, and be flexible along the way, never losing focus on what the end objective is. Running about at breakneck speed will not necessarily achieve anything, unless you have planned to ensure that all your effort is geared to the right audience, at the right time, with the right message.

Relationship marketing
People are very wary of those who suddenly become their best friend to achieve a marketing objective and then disappear until they need something again. A lot of your long-term marketing benefit will come from people you deal with time and again who trust you.

Who are you focusing on?
I am trying to get you to work on your self-promotion; however, I must also urge you to do this with your focus on others. Are you constantly trying to give your audience / clients what they want? You may need to demonstrate clearly you have done it but really making the marketing philosophy part of your belief system will pay dividends.

It is obvious if you have your own business to take this focus but, even if you work within an organisation, it is important to think about all the people you are working with. Why are they dealing with you? What result are they looking for? And what impact can your activities have? Could you do anything more to make a greater contribution?

If you want to do work for a new customer, find an opportunity to do something on a small scale to demonstrate your worth.

Always deliver
Whatever marketing activity you can undertake, whoever you are marketing to, one of your key messages should be that you will always deliver what you promise. This will shock people, as it turns the normal strategy of "over-promise / under-deliver" on its head.

Learn from companies
Look at how major brands achieve success – what is it about NIKE or McDonalds, etc., that make you want to use them, rather than the opposition? How can you use this in your own case? What strategies worked for them and might work for you in a different setting?

Testing
You may not be a business, but it is always important to test what is working for you. Where is your profile coming from? What are you getting out of it? You need to track responses, but also the difference between people who have noticed, and those who have actively engaged with you, as a result of your marketing.

The whole concept of personal marketing is not just to get some recognition of you as a brand but also tangible results. Following Pareto's Law (a favourite of mine, I know), 20% of your activities will yield 80% of your results, and you have to increase these priorities.

Look at the different events that can yield results. They may be presentations, e-mails, your attendance at events, your online profile – which is working for you? Can you change your approach a little in each and measure the result? Small changes can be the leverage point to lead to overall significant improvement. The ability to break down each process and measure the changes is useful.

TASK 4.5

How do you market yourself? Break down the process. Set up a system to measure the performance of each element.

Endorsement
The endorsement of key influencers will always play a significant part in building your profile.

Relationships
Systematically building relationships with other people and organisations where you will actively seek information and help each other is always useful. Always try to contribute to other people you want to work with even before a deal is struck. You need to look formally for referrals or chances to do interesting projects. Always be willing to help anyone within your organisation with new projects. Who could be a key influencer in your career and what could you contribute to help them with their performance?

If you own a business, you are attempting to find the ideal customer who needs the benefits that your products or services can bring. Clarity in knowing the end customer, their needs and what particular problems they have are vital before you design a product or service to meet those needs / problems. The same applies internally within an organisation or a community.

When someone is running a business, most people can accept the need for a formalised referral process. Some will feel this is a manipulative process, likened to "office politics" by some in the corporate world. I have often sympathised with this viewpoint, however, we are talking about you achieving your goals and being the best you can be. If you leave things to chance, there will be no correlation between your performance and your rewards. If you refuse to market yourself personally, you are not making other people aware of what you can do and are less likely to be given an opportunity to work with them. It is up to you.

Clients or contacts you have lost
You will find out the hard way in business that you will have disagreements with people, both internally and externally, no matter how good your intentions. The key is to part as amicably as possible and to keep in touch. You, your position or your circumstances may have changed, so later it could be useful to get in touch again and to try to rebuild the relationship. If you have not already dealt with the cause of the disagreement, now is the time to do so.

Other promotional tools
How do you keep people informed about what you are up to now? Direct mail and / or email in an organised fashion can keep you in touch with your client base.

Go through your contacts

Sit down and go through your contacts, internal and external. Divide them into appropriate categories. You want to find the people who either themselves need benefits you can offer or who know people who do. You are trying to find trends or connections in order to be as efficient as you can – so, if three accountants you know all need upskilling in their personal communication skills, perhaps other accountants will too. Above all realise you do have a lot to offer. How can you do more? How can you reach more people or make an impact? Use marketing to help as many people as possible and be the best you can be.

Since you do not have the time or resources to launch a full-time campaign, you must apply Pareto's law and get the 80% of results that 20% of your time can identify.

Decide also what is the best strategy to approach the people you identify. It may be a short email or written note, which should be followed by a phone call. As someone who uses email extensively, I know you must guard against the tonality of your emails. And recognise that there will be many cases where a phone call or a face-to-face meeting are the only way to make things happen.

Your own website

I am not saying that it is strictly necessary in every case to have a personal website but, with a good marketing strategy to drive either the internal traffic on an intranet or outside traffic, websites do have a significant part to play in your marketing. The creation of a virtual community with similar interests to you not only yields potential profitable business but also provides research advice and ongoing learning. The use of search engines and possibly a number of sites for each niche can be considered. A small company I know has 24 different websites, aimed at 24 different niches.

The other key potential of a website is that you can reach out on a global basis, without leaving your office. Potential business from the new emerging economies can be obtained that way.

Creative marketing budget

If you have little money available to invest in your marketing, it could be useful to offer some of your products / services in return for marketing help.

Keeping in contact

You can see there are so many things to do. How do you maintain contact with all these people? What you need to do, once you have made your list, is to set up a simple system that will allow you to stay in touch. You and anyone who helps have to do this with sincerity, otherwise your effort will be wasted.

A marketing plan

You need a plan with a set of goals and measurable events towards an end product. Again, it is what you do on a weekly basis, rather than in a once-a-blitz year, that will determine whether your marketing strategies are a success. It is too easy, if things are going well with one strategy, or if you are too busy, not to work systematically. However, that forms the basis of your work, your feedback and marketing strategies. Whether you work for a company or run your own company, marketing is a key life skill. It will decide ultimately how successful your career or business is. Devote at least three hours per week to marketing, much more if you are in business.

It may not seem that important but I remember, as a businessman, trying to set up one afternoon a week for marketing. However, I didn't do it, as I had so much work on and, as "time is money", I wanted to invoice as much as possible. I came to regret it later because my positioning suffered.

One last thought: Marketing is for life!

5

FEAR OF FINANCE

"SHOW ME THE MONEY"

Money makes the world go around and I want to convince you to take it seriously. People either are obsessed by money or completely disregard it. This is not helped by the fact that, up until now, there has been virtually no money education in schools and, at university, only students who study it are bamboozled with a mix of complex formulae and jargon that sends them off to sleep and lack of understanding. I have found chief executives who cry when they have to look at a financial report and have met accountants and bank managers who have no idea how to build wealth.

Whatever your motivation, do not underestimate money. I do not want to turn you into a modern day Scrooge, who, despite vast wealth, makes no contribution and lives a miserable existence, always wanting more. Scrooge still exists, you know. I met a 65-year-old man who had worked for a multi-millionaire for 20 years as a van-driver, being paid barely the minimum wage. When I asked the old gent why he was bringing the case, he explained that the previous year, after 19 years of employment, his boss had told him he was buying him Christmas dinner for the first time. Touched by this kind gesture, he noticed the next morning that something had been posted through his letter box at his house. When he opened the door, there was a chicken leg, wrapped up in tin-foil – his Christmas dinner! Needless to say, he wasn't impressed and sued.

However, money does play a significant part, even if you are involved in an organisation that does not have the profit motive. Community organisations spend a great deal of their time starved of resources and public sector organisations now have to be accountable financially.

Many people have a phobia about money, accounts and anything to do with numbers. Usually it starts with difficulty with maths at school and the creation of a fundamental belief, "I hate numbers, I'm crap at maths and will never be able to handle money"! I find it hard to understand the problem at times as much of maths consists of the ability to add up, multiply and divide, using a calculator. That is all you have to learn to do, and I promise you will have a greater understanding of money and the part it will play in your life. What is important is not only that you understand the part it plays in business / community ventures, but also what your financial aims are.

The reality

The reality is that you will spend a substantial part of your life working, either to make or to earn money to fund your life and that of your loved ones and to provide for your retirement.

Those of you at university may feel that money does not matter and that community issues and doing what you enjoy is all that is important. But, in today's financial climate for students, where student loans and part-time jobs are the norm, what I want is to help you to make your decisions with an understanding of money and what the future holds.

Do I want wealth?

I recognise that your priorities will change, but it is important to think where you want to end up. That interesting post in the civil service may appear attractive now, after years of student penny-pinching, but there is one thing for sure, you will never become seriously wealthy in the civil service. Public sector jobs offer index-linked pensions and challenging work, but these are not a path to financial independence. You may be happy to get a public sector job now, but you may evolve into someone who, in 10 or 15 years' time, realises they wanted a different financial reality. Maybe you can leave and set up your own business but the odds are against you after years of pubic sector working and a secure job, and the commitments you will probably have gathered up. Please do not misunderstand me. I simply want you to try to make a strategic decision and go into the world of work with your eyes open.

If wealth is something you would like to have, private enterprise is the best chance. Certain professions are also more likely than others to provide significant income opportunities, though most will more likely to lead to financial comfort rather than wealth and financial freedom. Dentists, doctors, lawyers and accountants are amongst those who should do comfortably.

Parental values I understand as one myself. You want your child to have an enjoyable and worthwhile career, as you may have had (or not had!)

yourself. You don't really want your child to face the uncertainty of self-employment and entrepreneurship. You notice that the local dentist or lawyer tend to live in bigger houses, drive BMWs and have a good lifestyle, while entrepreneurs tend to have more up and downs. You then subtly encourage little Johnnie to go down that path. Forgive us, our intentions are good but based on certain false premises.

Do what you love

If you genuinely like something, you will show lots of interest and take extra care in your work. Normally, this will lead to excellent performance. I do subscribe to a certain extent to the dictate "Do what you love and the money will follow". If you choose psychology as your area to specialise in, this may not be recognised as highly in the "parental professional status" stakes. However, if you are a very good psychologist, with some of the E-Factor skills outlined here, particularly personal marketing, you can do very well. However, this is where an understanding of business / finance matters because you can easily take a different road. Many of the psychology jobs available are in the public sector and, if you do not take an enterprising approach to your career development, you an easily end up in a situation which only the most enterprising or innovative will escape. The brilliant psychology graduate at 21 can end up at 36 married with two children, an educational psychologist for the civil service, all because of the initial route he or she chose. Please don't think I am demeaning this path, I just want you to make career and business decisions based on your long-term financial values and goals. So do what you love, but make sure you are enterprising enough to know where you want to end up and to consider taking options that open up possibilities at a later date.

The same applies to companies. If you are a mechanical engineer and you spend the first 10 years of your career in the cigarette manufacturing industry, you may well become an expert in cigarette machinery. This is not transferable to other industries and you have committed your career to what is essentially a declining industry, due to worldwide trends. Think ahead!

EMPLOYMENT OR SELF-EMPLOYMENT

I want you to be as enterprising as possible. Therefore, I should be recommending self employment. However, there are advantages and disadvantages.

Being honest, employment with a large multinational will offer a lot of benefits that self-employment or employment with a community office cannot. You know exactly where you are financially and, therefore, can plan more easily for savings, mortgages, etc. However, you will pay PAYE, which means income tax and national / social insurance will be deducted from your gross pay at source, with very little room for expenses or allowances. This means that as regards net income, you will be worse off earning the same gross income as a self-employed person, who may be able to deduct expenses from their before-tax income. What I do advise you to do, whether as a self-employed person or an employee, is to see yourself as a "provider of services" and to make sure you are getting the best possible return, both financially and in terms of career prospects and professional development.

Having attended a recent Scottish Institute of Enterprise conference, I was pleased to see that a number of major corporation employers are actually looking for employees with the skills that form part of the E-Factor.

In making your career decision at this stage, look at where a long-term career path with an organisation can lead financially. It may be difficult for you to assess this at this stage. Being a managing director, earning £150,000, for a major company can seem like a dream, when you have just finished your daily shift at McDonalds at £4.15 per hour. However, remember that it costs £750,000 to buy a decent house in London and, as an employee, the managing director's £150,000 is approximately £75,000 net, just over £6,000 a month. Add a couple of kids and a spouse at home, plus the 70 hours a week the job demands, and the position is not quite as attractive as it first appears. However, for the enterprising, if the company has a good training programme and offers significant early opportunities for training and responsibility, an entry position there is a chance to learn some of your mistakes in a safe environment. I am all for "the school of hard knocks" but too many knocks too early in your career could put you out of the running for a long time.

I am one of those people whose mission in life is to encourage other people – in particular, graduates – to start their own business, particularly a global business. However, let's look at the financial advantages and disadvantages of self-employment. Having done that I will give you a strategy, whatever route you choose.

Financial advantages of self-employment

One of the biggest advantages is the tax implications. A self-employed person is able to claim a much greater range of expenses against his / her taxable income than an employee. Let us take the case of a chartered surveyor earning gross income of £50,000 and compare their situation as employed or self-employed. The employee will pay approximately 50% of their income in income tax and national / social insurance. Not only does the self-employed person pay virtually no national insurance, saving almost £5,000, they also are able to claim as deductible all sorts of expenses – for example, the running costs of the car used for business, travel, a spouse's wages if he / she helps with the business, going to exhibitions, indeed anything that could be related to pursuing the business – this might knock off in net tax terms up to another £5,000. Quite significant! Now it's not always this straightforward but there is a significant tax advantage in being self-employed.

There is also no cap on your income. You charge what you are worth. You are only limited by the time you can spend and what your client will pay. There is no limit to this, if your business is providing information or products. You also can hopefully make money by employing people who work for you.

Disadvantages

These are the key financial disadvantages of being self-employed. First, cash flow – your ability to pay your bills and reinvest in your business, as well as pay yourself a salary, is determined by when your clients pay you. Meanwhile, you may be relying on your bank manager to help you pay your creditors unless your creditors will give you a similar payment time period to your customers.

Next, as a self-employed person, the price you pay for reduced or no national / social insurance is the inability to claim benefits from the state should you fall sick or be unable to work.

And you might find it harder to raise a personal loan or mortgage, since your income is not always certain but depends on how well your business does each year.

Last, there's risk. You risk financial failure in running your own enterprise, since you operate in an uncertain environment. Arguably, this risk exists in large companies, even in traditionally safe sectors such as banking, but it's not a personally-assumed risk, not to the same extent.

Conclusion

Whether you are ready to run your own enterprise is up to you. There is lots of support available out there and, to be honest, you can cut down your personal risk with limited company status (see **The Streetwise Guide to Starting Your Own Business**). However, some of the enterprise skills I am trying to teach you in this book will be learned more effectively in running your own business.

There are various halfway-house solutions. Start a part-time enterprise, as long as it is not against your employer's rules, create a tax loss and set it against your PAYE tax. Even a part-time venture will yield a lot of the lessons and make you "streetwise".

Sign up for any type experiential learning that aims to allow you to do things, so that you can experience the rollercoaster of business in a safe environment. An example of this is the TV reality show "The Apprentice", where the contestants get a lot of chances to put into practice the skills we are talking about here.

Although there is no doubt that there is nothing like the real thing, I am not saying you have got to set up a large business and take all the risks, but what is important is that you treat community, as well as business, ventures as financial challenges and learn financial reality through your experiences.

Also be clever enough to learn from both successful and unsuccessful business people. If I was going to give you another enterprise skill, it would be to learn continuously.

So let's continue Finance 101. If you can make these part of your behaviours, they will serve you well wherever you end up.

TASK 5.1

Have a go at setting out your financial goals. What would you like to be earning in a year, five years, 10 years? What type of lifestyle would you like to lead?

BUSINESS FINANCE

Handling money in your own venture demands certain skills / disciplines, because of the uncertainty and risk of business. These skills are also very applicable to corporate / community ventures and, indeed, to your personal finances. Get the fundamentals right and it will help your chance of making your enterprise work.

Cash is king

The first thing you need to learn, and it's counter-intuitive, is that cash flow, as opposed to profit, dictates the survival of a business. You can be making money on paper but, if it is not there in the bank when you have to pay bills, you are potentially insolvent at that moment.

Let me illustrate this – you have been running your own business for the past three months. Your sales were £1,000 in month 1, £2,000 in month 2 and £3,000 in month 3 – and you have had to pay expenses of £1,500 every month. Even though your total sales to date are £6,000 and your expenses only £4500, giving you a profit of £1,500 (not bad for your first three months!), you are facing cash flow problems, because your customers pay you two months after the date of the sale.

Profit & loss account	Month 1	Month 2	Month 3
Sales	1,000	2,000	3,000
Expenses	1,500	1,500	1,500
Profit	(500)	500	1,500
Cash flow statement	**Month 1**	**Month 2**	**Month 3**
Cash IN	0	0	1,000
Cash OUT	(1,500)	(1,500)	(1,500)
Net cash flow	(1,500)	(1,500)	(500)
Opening cash balance	0	(1,500)	(3,000)
Net cash flow (above)	(1,500)	(1,500)	(500)
Closing cash balance	(1,500)	(3,000)	(2,500)

The business will gradually catch up on its cash flow, as your sales are more than expenses but, at the moment, you can't pay your bills without the help of the bank. This is why planning your financial budget is important but particularly so for businesses, so that you can cover the periods when cash flow will be slow. You have also got to be tough at credit control, making sure you get paid as soon as possible. All businesses / organisations pay lots of bills; if they think you are relaxed about when you get paid, guess who goes to the back of the queue! Spell out your credit terms and adopt a fair, but firm, policy. Otherwise, even when you are making money, it will be in your creditor's bank account and not your own where it should be.

TASK 5.2

Look at your financial budget, personal or business, for the next six months. Are you sure enough is coming in to meet outgoings? How can you plan for this?

Profit

Although cash flow is vital to keep bills paid, it is important to realise that you are in business to make a profit and, even as a community or public sector organisation, you do not want a deficit and want to break even at least. Believe it or not, you can get so busy doing the work and running an operation that you will lose track as to why you are in business.

Stuart Wilde, an author on spiritual enlightenment, launched a worldwide business a number of years ago. As you can imagine, the people who ran his companies were more interested in their karma or spirituality rather than the performance of the business. Like Stuart, they wanted to save the world. However, as he gradually realised his business was not performing, Stuart Wilde hit on a novel way of letting his managers understand the realities of business. He would ring them once a day, every day, and ask "How many, how much?", and then slam the phone down. After two weeks, they got the message. Stuart wanted to know how many books they were selling each day, and how much their turnover was. The business changed as their attitude changed. They still wanted to save the world, but they knew they had to make the business viable to do this. If you are in business, no matter what contribution you make, you are in it to make and collect the money.

There is no other reason to be in business other than this. Lose sight of this and you will be in trouble.

Even in community or public sector organisations where you may not have the profit motive, you are judged on the efficiency of your operation and future funding and budgets depend on this.

I still don't want you to make money your only goal but you have got to operate within financial constraints and handle money or it will handle you!!

Pricing margin

Getting your pricing right and controlling your costs in line with this margin at appropriate volume levels are key variables in whether a venture will work or not. Ideally, you want as good a margin as you can get. You should only sacrifice margin for a large enough volume of work.

Whether you are running your own business or working for a company, you should always measure the return you are getting for the effort put in. Remember, whether self-employed or employed, you are giving your skills for an adequate return. Every hour you spend working is an hour with an opportunity lost.

So get an appropriate price. As a business, you need to remember that you have to recover both direct and indirect costs.

Pricing is also a psychological area. How much do you value yourself and your contribution / product? There is no point quoting a price of £1,000 per day for your work for a community enterprise with a maximum budget of £500 per day. However, perhaps you could contribute in another way or work in another market where there are financial rewards appropriate for your contribution.

Particularly with personal services, there is an element of what you charge is the worth you attribute to yourself. I am sad to disillusion you but heed the old truism that "if you don't value yourself, nobody else will". If you are willing to sell your services for a cup of coffee, that is all the other party will offer.

The bottom line

"The bottom line is relentless". Gaining some financial knowledge will help you make decisions. You must be sure you are getting your profit margins, or in a community project meeting the financial criteria set.

Income should exceed expenditure go!

You have always to act according to your means. It is important to dress well and act the part of where you want to end up, but not if it involves taking on massive financial commitments you are not ready for. For instance, even though you feel you need to drive a 7 series BMW, it's probably not appropriate (or affordable!) as a trainee architect.

Keeping your head

Again, if your small business starts to go well and you suddenly have money in the bank, or have got a substantial salary increase, this can be a defining moment. Can you do a Rudyard Kipling and "treat triumph and disaster just the same"? It goes without saying that keeping a cool head when you are in financial difficulty is important and obvious. Equally hard, though, is keeping your head when things seem to be taking off. With self employment, in particular, even if your business is riding high at present, there is no guarantee that it will be in the next calendar year. You will also be liable to pay approximately tax on your profits to the taxman at the end of the year, so put some aside for tax and for re-investment and, then by all means enjoy the rest of it.

FINANCIAL DOCUMENTS

It is important that you understand the key financial documents – cash flow statement, profit and loss account, and the balance sheet – whether you are either an entrepreneur (actual or would-be), or an enterprising corporate or community person, as doing so will advance your career. Arguably, using the documents as a tool for personal financial planning can help you achieve your own financial goals, too.

Profit and loss account

Let us do a simple profit and loss for one year. Let's say you run a restaurant.

Profit and loss account	£
Sales	300,000
Cost of Sales	150,000
Gross Profit	150,000
Running Expenses	135,000
Net profit	15,000

The profit and loss measures your gross margin after the manufacture of your product and the net margin after all claimed expenses.

Your gross margin is calculated as:

$$\frac{150,000}{300,000} \quad \frac{\text{gross profit}}{\text{sales}} \quad = \quad 50\%$$

Every time you spend 50p making and selling the product, you make £1, which is the average for the restaurant industry.

Your net margin is calculated as:

$$\frac{15,000}{300,000} \quad \frac{\text{net profit}}{\text{sales}} \quad = \quad 5\%$$

Every time, you have £1 of sales, you generate 5p of net profit.

Your profit and loss account includes all sales, whether paid or not, and all running costs, whether paid or not. So, as we saw earlier, you can make a profit on paper – but, if the cash flow is not right, you can still be struggling.

The gross margin above is really a test of operational efficiency. The net margin reflects whether the overheads or running costs are in line with the net profit. Again, whether in business or personal life, it is very easy for costs to exceed income and, in particular, to exceed available cash flow.

Money spent unnecessarily is opportunity missed for savings, business and long-term strategies. However I don't want you to turn out to be like a certain 70-year-old multi-millionaire I met recently, who was almost in tears telling me he could only now afford to go to Scotland due to easyJet's low airfares. I don't think he was getting the full benefit of his money.

The balance sheet

The balance sheet is a snapshot of what you or the business is worth at any one particular moment in time.

For example, you are a 40-year-old male. You own your own house worth £200,000 and have £20,000 savings in the bank. You have a mortgage of £100,000 on the house. Your personal balance sheet today looks like this:

Balance sheet	£
Assets	
House	200,000
Savings	20,000
Total Assets	220,000
Liabilities	
Mortgage	100,000
Net Worth	120,000

You have assets worth £220,000 but owe £100,000 against them. After paying all your bills, you are worth £120,000.

The key to long-term financial success, either as an individual or a business, is to build a strong balance sheet. A pension is ultimately an asset, a sum of money from which eventually you can have an income or buy an income-producing asset such as a business property or other investment in time or money.

Some people are lucky to be given shareholdings in lucrative family businesses or property portfolios. For the rest of us, it is necessary to build a portfolio of assets. For those of you, particularly in the public sector or major corporate entity, you will be focused on establishing a pension. Nothing wrong with that, except in most cases, due to the changes in population, etc., schemes don't offer a guaranteed excellent return. Therefore, you should think about building some assets for yourself to lessen your risk and give you a better return.

The danger of having a high-powered job at, say, £100,000 a year, or a small business making you the same, is that you are unlikely to build assets unless you set out to do so. With the job, hopefully you will have some type of pension scheme; as a self-employed person, you will have a better net income due to tax advantages but, in either case, if you pretty much live a lifestyle that matches your income and don't create a surplus that you use in an enterprising and innovative way, you are likely to struggle financially in a long-term basis.

TASK 5.3

Draw up your own balance sheet now. Be honest. It is not where you are now that's important but where you are going to end up. Check your balance sheet at least once per year. The better the balance sheet, the greater freedom you have to do what you want. To increase it, you have to be strategic, something which is very hard when you are young and which can look pointless when you are old.

FINANCIAL STRATEGY

Being strategic is looking beyond the next five years. To get where you want to be in the long-term, recognise that the decisions you make now will have consequences in the long-run. Unfortunately, both business and individuals seem to vary between the cost-conscious Scrooge-type to the party animal who, whatever he makes, spends more. Some people get confused as to how pop stars and celebrities or even business people who earn millions can end up with nothing. Simple, they gross a million, on which they owe, say, £400,000 tax. They party and spend the million and next year, as can happen in any business, they earn very little. The problem is they still owe £400,000 tax, and have no money to pay it, and no money to sustain their new lifestyle.

Before you think I am turning into a bore, I do appreciate a quote attributed to George Best, a former Northern Ireland footballer, who made his way through a few millions in his time: "I spent most of it on wine, women and parties, I wasted the rest" he is reported to have said. The question from an elderly porter in an Edinburgh hotel, on bringing champagne to Best's room when he was staying playing matches for Hibernian – Best had just won £10,000 in the hotel's casino and was sitting with ex-Miss World Mary Stavi, his then girlfriend – "Mr Best, where did it all go wrong?" is another classic.

The answer is to have a strategy. If you have a business, try to reinvest a portion of the profits.

I don't want you to become an accountant. I wouldn't recommend it. I believe you should be taking calculated risks and accountants, like bank managers, tend to be very good at analysing things, tearing them apart and rejecting them. They often count the beans for the successful enterpriser / E-Factor person, but rarely are the enterpriser themselves. However, you should take on board their good qualities. When you are spending money, it is good not to get too emotionally attached to material things, otherwise you will buy them when you can't afford them or pay too big a price for them. For example, you see a flat that you want, priced at £100,000. Your friend, an estate agent, says it is a good buy at £100,000 but no more. The bidding at auction goes up to £130,000 and you still try to buy it. You are "emotionally attached" to buying something at the wrong price – and emotions in business cause mistakes!

Cash flow forecasting / budgeting

Not another financial document. I knew it! He is trying to turn us into an accountant after all!

No, it is simply that it is a good idea, particularly for a business, to plan ahead for income and expenditure and identify when the cash is likely to come in and go out of the business. The timing of cash flow can play an important part in your success. Sod's law dictates that all your major bills will become due when income is unlikely to be available for banking. You may need to arrange overdraft facilities to ensure you don't have a financial "melt down" situation. Plan ahead and make sure you can deal with financial uncertainty.

If you are not keeping within the budget, at an early stage you need to take corrective action to get back on track. It is a bit late as a businessperson to realise you are having money problems because the bank is returning your cheques. This is crucial for a business and still important as an individual. There are some simple software systems available that can roll out budgets, based on entering a few statistics. Use a budget to keep track, enjoy yourself but without compromising your financial strategy.

Here is what a budget should look like. Don't be dazzled by the reams of figures. It is simply a list of your planned spending and income receipts over the period of the budget.

Jayne's Consultancy: Cash budget for six months to (date)

Cash budget	M 1	M 2	M 3	M 4	M 5	M 6
	£	£	£	£	£	£
Income	0	0	0	2,000	3,000	2,000
Expenditure:						
Costs	1,000	1,000	1,000	1,000	1,000	1,000
Salary	1,000	1,000	1,000	1,000	1,000	1,000

TASK 5.4

Based on the figures above, how big is Jayne's cash flow problem? (The answer is in Appendix 2.)

Conclusion

Money is only a resource to be used so that you can develop a business and live your life to the fullest. Unfortunately, many people are unable to handle money and it takes away from their enjoyment of life. What I am warning you is that, unless you go and live in a cave, it is very difficult to avoid money. Let us say you despise business, you want to do good and go and work for a charity. As their manager, what will be the first document you look at that will govern how you run the charity? Yes, the budget. You have to live within your funding to keep the community work going. For me, it is simply a tool which, carefully used, can enhance the contribution of your business and help you do what you want with your life. Handling money cleverly is part of the enterprising person's make-up. They may look for specialist financial advice when required, but they usually consider the financial consequences of their decisions and make the right moves to get what they want. I quite respect those of you who, unlike me, refuse to contemplate becoming a millionaire. However, money can play such a part in blocking business start-up or growth. Many good people end up working 40 hours a week just to live a fairly mundane life.

I feel if you have an enterprising / innovative capacity, you should have a chance to apply this, to live life and to help others. Don't let the lack of key financial strategies hold you back!

RAISING MONEY

Any enterprise business or community has to raise money to start up, grow and / or survive.

My belief is that, if the project is good enough, there will be money available for it somewhere; your job is to find it and to persuade the funders to back you. This applies, even if you work within a large company, where senior managers will have to agree to include your project within their budgets.

In raising funds, your personal influence and marketing skills will help in building your financial acumen and results. You will quickly realise that not every one will agree to back you. For instance, let's say you are opening a new juice bar in your local town. You have just graduated and you ask your local bank manager to lend you £5,000 and he says "No". For some people, the rejection is a real blow and they give up on the idea of starting their own business. The reality is that, as a young person with no capital and no assets for the bank manager to secure the loan against, you are a bad risk. However, if you do your research, you will find there are specialist loan and grant schemes available to help people under 30 start their own business, as well as a range of other options available.

What will funders want to know?

They will want to see your business plan and budget and will want to know why you need the money. However, not only the business model is being evaluated, your ability to manage is also under review. Will you stick at it? Will you be able to sell your product or service and make the business happen? So getting the funds can be very much a selling exercise, both on paper and in person.

Debt

There is good debt and bad debt. Loans to buy a range of consumer goods are only to be recommended on a limited basis; some type of mortgage for property and a possible car loan are also acceptable. Too much consumer debt can mean you have to work 40 hours a week simply to service your loans and credit card debt.

Innovation financing
Ideally, you should always be looking for creativity in finding your funding for projects and personal ventures. Obviously, it is a good idea to see if any grants are available, as this is free money that does not have to be repaid. There are lots of funds available, if you search and check that you can meet the funders' criteria.

Private investors

I am not recommending that you sell part of your family home to someone else but, in business ventures, not enough enterprisers look for investment from outsiders. There are lots of outside "business angels", successful business people who want to invest money in ventures with a possible long term return or even in community ventures that meet their strategic charity obligations.

Leverage

I want to introduce you to the concept of "leverage". This is making money or achieving results using other people's money, time or resources. It does sound like the original "capitalist" concept: get the factors of production, work them into shape whatever the consequences and keep all the "filthy lucre" yourself. However it is not that. Unless you are a popstar, famous sportsperson or a very exceptional chief executive, there is a limit to what you can achieve in your own time. If you are going to set up a charity, unless you are already wealthy, you are going to have to use someone else's money to fund your project and the time of volunteers to make it happen.

Ideally, in today's environment, I would always recommend that you try to use leverage wherever you can. You have only a limited time and you do not want to work all the hours available just to get by because you have a private life, family and friends who need some of your time and you need to preserve a work / life balance to have the best possible life to cope with stress and to keep healthy. It can be a quality of the enterprising person to want to do everything to make sure it is done right. However, using other resources can be much more effective.

I am suggesting you do this with the utmost integrity. There have been companies and politicians who have achieved wealth through the use of their countries' resources, However, use the leverage of others, ideally on a win-

win basis, or you will find that other people will be using your time to leverage their own projects, whether in business or within an organisation.

RATIOS

One of the key areas any business person has to consider is ratios. These are a set of statistics based on financial statements. We have already talked about some of them, gross margin on sales, net margin, etc. If you can understand balance sheets and profit and loss accounts, you can measure the return on the worth of your business. Let us say your business' balance sheet shows a bottom line figure of £100,000 but it only makes you £5,000 a year, that is not a good return on your investment.

In making decisions financially, it depends on the ratios. If you buy a property, for instance, which may look very well or be in Spain, your favourite holiday destination, what is most important is whether the deal makes sense. What did you pay against market value? When you add up all the costs against the return adjusted for periods without a tenant, is it still a good deal? If it isn't, walk away. Business is a numbers game. If you only look at one deal or one customer, you tie yourself in. If you wanted to buy or start a business, you should look at least 100, until you see the right business or right deal for you. The same applies to looking for a job.

TAXES

Taxes can be a very substantial drain on building your wealth portfolio. However, in most countries, tax is the key source of government income and it is the law that you pay your share. I am certainly not recommending tax evasion, which is against the law. But tax avoidance, where you plan your financial affairs to lessen tax liabilities, needs to be considered. Let us say you have written a book and you have been offered £80,000 as a lump sum advance. The book has taken you five years to write and you probably won't write another one (don't worry, I will!). This £80,000 one-off lump sum could prove to be a substantial part of your investment portfolio and long-term retirement income. It is perfectly reasonable to plan to limit your tax liability

– for instance, by operating within a company and making a substantial tax-deductible self-administered pension fund payment.

Plan for tax

If you are self-employed, you need to decide to plan ahead for tax and get yourself the best deal without breaking the law. Limited companies can be very advantageous tax vehicles for growth businesses.

For employees, there can be significant tax advantages in having a part-time business that could claim expenses and provide potential tax rebate situations.

The important thing with tax is to be strategic. Before making any financial decision, you should have a review with your tax adviser.

As an enterprising individual with financial skills, you will always consider the tax angle as part of your decision. However, if you want to be based in the UK or the USA, you will always have some tax liability and need to accept that the most important thing financially is to make your margin and get paid. Getting used to setting aside 25% of the profits for tax provision is a good habit.

THE PERSON YOU ARE

The fascinating thing I found out by working in a bank and as an accountant is that it is the habits you have rather than your income which matter. You see people earning £60,000 per year and spending £62,000 and people earning £10,000 a year and saving £2,000 and buying commercial property.

You might dismiss this chapter as the ramblings of a boring accountant (you may be right!). But what I want to do is to save you from some of the financial heartache I have experienced, not because I didn't have financial qualifications (I became a qualified accountant and financial planner), but because having qualifications does not guarantee you have the competences and will act in the best way for yourself. A lot of the points I am making came from financial mistakes I made.

Be clear about what you want to do financially. Do you want to be wealthy? If so, at what level? What lifestyle do you want? Have you the right plan to get what you want? What are you prepared to sacrifice to get this?

Like all the E-Factors, there is no better learning place than in the game of life. The next time you have a financial decision to make, look at it differently.

My advice is to make money and use it wisely for your own freedom, your family and to help the community.

As one famous business person said, "Once you get money out of the way, then you can be good". Get it out of the way by treating it with respect and have the right strategies so that it helps you do what you want with your life. We never found out what happened to the new Scrooge in "A Christmas Carol", after he started treating people well and helping others. That did not make him a fool, but wealth and the ability to handle money whether as a business person or manager is a key requisite of the job and, if you want to take part, essential to enjoying your life in this commercial world. Why don't you "show me the money" and complete the task below to show you have got what it takes.

TASK 5.5

Pick your own business or where you work. What will you have to do to be financially independent in 10 years? What financial changes do you need to make?

6

INFLUENCE

It is important to realise that none of your business, career or life plans will come to fruition, unless you get other people to support your ideas. You need to convince other people that your ideas / projects will work and that you are the person to deliver them. So you need to influence / persuade others to back you. Influencing consists of a number of individual skills that we will examine in this chapter, all of which are important in delivering results:

- Communication skills.
- Networking skills.
- Selling / negotiating skills.

Unfortunately, like many of the other enterprise skills, you are not taught these in any standard school or university course. However, you can acquire them, if you are prepared to learn the basic transferable skills but, above all, if you are prepared to apply and practice them in your every day life.

COMMUNICATION

Are you a good communicator? Other people need to be aware of your ideas / projects and you need to interact with other people to make things happen – this is why communication is so important. You are constantly communicating whether you realise it or not. Communication is much more than just speaking or the written word. Your body language, your tonality, what you do, what you wear, all communicate a message to others. You communicate non-verbally as well as verbally and, unless you get it right, you are unlikely to be as effective a communicator as you could be.

Be a listener

Ironically, although I am trying to help you to be better at getting your ideas across to persuade other people, one of the key communication skills is listening. By "listening", I really don't mean pretending to be interested, I mean genuinely to take time to listen to other people, as Covey says "to understand before being understood", taking the time to understand where the other person is coming from, whether you agree with them or not. Everyone has a story to tell and a point to make. You will diffuse arguments, and have a better chance of persuading others, if you can respect other people and their viewpoints. Do it with sincerity or don't do it at all. I am not saying that, if you are at a party and you are cornered by the party "bore", you have to sit there in rapt attention for hours on end. However, be genuinely interested in others and what they have got to say, and you will never know what you might learn!

Students who go for management assessment job interviews with large corporates often try to get their point across to "boss" the group. What they don't realise is that the students who listen to others and understand where the group is going before they say anything are the ones who are noticed - positively. They are seen as having the best potential. Why? Listening is a key skill. You need to understand your customer, friend, supplier or family member, and their priorities, before you attempt to gain their support or influence. Sincerity is everything both to learn and to communicate. *Now* are you listening?

The communication mix

Research shows that communication consists of 5% words, 40% body language and 55% tonality. People pick up on your non-verbal communication. Does what you do, your body language and your tonality all give the same message?

For instance, I met an old acquaintance this morning in a coffee shop. I asked him how he was and what he was doing. He said he was freelancing, while looking for the right position. However his flat tonality, lack of enthusiasm and poor posture / body movement told me he was in bad form and that things were not going too well. Am I a mind-reader? Unfortunately not, I'm just saying that was the message he was giving me, intentional or not. I could have put some work his way but the message I got was of someone in turmoil, not ready to undertake with enthusiasm and commitment the project work I needed done.

Physiology

An Israeli psychologist showed that there was a strong link between mind / body, and that movement could improve your state. If you stood up straight, looked up and moved with greater energy, your mood would improve.

Try it! Do you feel any better?

Let's say you are going in to meet your bank manger to seek funds for your new business. If you move confidently, have good posture and give off a relaxed, yet confident and business-like demeanour, he / she will take you more seriously. What the bank manager is trying to assess is whether you believe in the project, and how you will react to pressure. I do understand that, in going into this situation, it is easy to feel nervous and give off anything but positive vibes. However there is a *secret*. By moving your body in the way that a confident person does, you first convince yourself that you feel confident, and then convince the bank manager that you feel confident and thus become the enterprising person the bank manager is looking for.

"Dragon's Den" is a television programme that allows would-be businesspeople to pitch their idea to a group of multimillionaires, the "dragons", with a view to persuading them to invest in their idea. The dragons are so-called because they usually tear both the ideas and the contestants apart, making for compulsive viewing, a bit like watching Christians being torn apart by lions in Ancient Rome. However, one contestant recently was a very quiet young lady, whose business consisted of fashion jewellery. She impressed me both by her ability to listen to the panel's criticisms but also by her relaxed, yet confident, demeanour. She stood confidently, listened respectfully and responded, not with aggression but with quiet confidence, her voice, posture and words showing a quiet belief and a willingness to listen to other people's viewpoints. The panel got the message, all respected her influencing skills and she won a major investor.

Tonality

Tonality refers to more than just the pitch or timbre of your voice, important though that is. Tonality often represents the subtle message behind the words, whether spoken or written.

Many of us use emails or texts nowadays for quick communication. Sometimes, communication by email only can deliver the wrong underlying message. As you can imagine, particularly in face-to-face discussions or over the telephone, voice tonality can play a very important part in the communication. One of the key weaknesses many people have is lack of variety in their tonality; so when you speak, vary your tonality, make sure you put enthusiasm in your voice and that the tonality, above all, represents what you feel. You all know when someone has been "cool" to you over the phone, not through the words used, but by the tonality in their voice.

Never underestimate the part tonality can play. Get it wrong and you can significantly dilute the success of your communication. When you say, "I believe this product will increase your sales", a potential customer will search for any sign that you do not believe what you are saying. The voice tone can give that message.

Communication styles

To communicate successfully, the most important thing is to be flexible. Different styles of communication are appropriate for different situations and for different people. Possibly, the key thing is to take your time, assess what is appropriate and respond appropriately. You may feel, "I talk very enthusiastically and, if they don't get the message, that is their fault". However, as part of your respect towards other people, you need to put over the message to the other party in a way that they will understand. As Richard Bandler, a famous communication specialist, said, "The meaning of communication is the response you get". So the responsibility is yours. Some people like "the big picture", some like the detail; your job as an influencer is to satisfy everyone.

Sensory systems

Neuro-language processing (NLP), one of the most popular communications models, works on the basis that everyone has a different view of the world. Some people are visual, looking for visual evidence to understand everything, some are auditory who like to hear things and some are into their feelings and like to touch physical evidence. Each group also use language related to their system: visual people talk about "getting the picture"; auditory like "the sound of things"; and, for the kinaesthetic people, things "feel right". Start listening to the language of people to see whether you can identify what approach they prefer. Visual people often speak quickly in a high-pitched voice and, obviously, are into how things look, including their physical appearance; auditory have great tonality in their voice; while kinaesthetics speak slowly, focusing on their feelings. Very interesting, you may say but, so what? The danger is that if you are dealing with someone who has a different primary sensory system to you, unless you are aware of this, you could be talking at different speeds and using different words, and hindering rather than helping the communication process.

Let us say you are a feelings person, presenting your findings on a project to your visual boss. You keep explaining how you have a good "gut feeling about the project". You speak slowly and talk about "grasping the opportunity". Visual boss gets impatient with your slow rate of speech and interrupts and wants to know "what the big picture is?". He comments that your PowerPoint slides are not colourful enough. Here you have a mismatch in sensory styles, leading to poor communication.

The good communicator, when making a speech, spends 60% of their time / effort on visuals, since visuals account for 60% of the population; they then add sounds, working on their speech and emphasis, and ensure that they provide detailed handouts for the kinaesthetics to grasp. They use all three types of language and, if presenting to one key individual, will do their best to identify and use their preferred system. Are they being calculating? Surely, you should just be yourself and people should take you as they find you. NO, that is haphazard. To communicate, you need to get your message across and thus you need to minimise the barriers to clear communication between both parties.

TASK 6.1

Listen to the words people use. What is important to them?
What do you notice?

The Outcome formula
With any communication, be clear as to the outcome you want to achieve. Learn to assess carefully both verbal and non-verbal signs as to whether you are getting what you want and change your style or method accordingly.

Rapport

A key part of what you are doing here is building rapport. This is not pretending to be someone's best friend or faking interest in something you are not interested in. It is trying to be sensitive so that the person you are talking to feels a sense of affinity and is prepared to talk to you, even if you are in an adversarial position – watching out for their sensory system helps, matching breathing tonality and body posture in a subtle way will help also.

Let me give you an example of this. You get a very angry customer on the phone. They start shouting, "This is the second time your company has let me down". Conventional customer services wisdom insists that you quietly calm them down. However, first, you have got to match their breathing and speech tonality, otherwise it will make them more angry. I don't mean that you shout loudly at them, but you have got to match them to get rapport before you gradually level them to a solution. Try it and see. I found this out by an accident with an aggressive client who never seemed to respond to my calming measures. He found out my home number and rang me on a Friday night about a fairly minor problem. As usual, he was sounding off. Unfortunately, or fortunately as it turned out, I answered his rather aggressive communication style in similar vein, simply because at 10 o'clock on a Friday night I could not be bothered to get into "calming down" mode. To my surprise, I built a much more effective rapport with my client than before, which continues to this day.

The basis of rapport is that people communicate better with people who are like them. That does not mean that you pretend to like, or be like, people you don't. However, if you need a communication process to take place with anyone, it is better to "be on the same wavelength". You need to show respect for how they communicate. This can include their style of presentation, the words they use, non-verbal clues, body language and even their cultural background.

Some people, the successful communicators, can do this effortlessly; you can do it too, and at least improve how you are doing, if you start to practice rapport building.

TASK 6.2

- Go into a pub or restaurant and watch groups of friends and couples. Watch to see any signs of rapport.
- Think of a difficult meeting you have coming up. Plan how you will build rapport with that person or group.
- Practice building rapport on a daily basis.

If you want to influence people, you must build rapport before you attempt to influence / persuade. Otherwise, lack of rapport will lead to a refusal to consider your point of view.

These skills need to be used with the best of intentions. If you use them, you will suddenly find a whole new world opening to you – watch out, though, you may have too much fun!

NETWORKING

The idea of deliberately meeting people socially with the prime purpose of advancing your career or business does not sit easily with some people. If it is done with the sole intention of using other people for your own ends, that is indeed shallow. However, building contacts who will be of help to you can be a fun process and should be an ongoing part of your business and personal life. If you are totally antisocial and refuse to speak to anyone other than a few close friends, you may get some "brownie points" – but, unless you are either vastly wealthy or hold some position of power already, accept the fact that you will be neither a business or social success unless you take on board the old truism, "It is not always what you know but who you know".

I am trying to improve your personal influence to help you achieve the results you want. I know that, in an ideal world, these results should be based solely on your abilities and hard work. Sadly, that is not the case. If you are really useless at your job or your business does not add value, your networks will not save you. However, they do provide significant advantages to anyone who will work at networking in a continuous, systematic way.

Why are networks so useful?

Networks are great fun. You will gain an understanding of a wide variety of areas. You will also learn a lot of informal information that would not reach you otherwise. You also will get to know a lot of people, who know people, who know people, who could make a huge difference to the outcome of your project or business. There is something known as "the power of 6", which is the concept that everyone in the world is only six people removed from anyone else through the power of networking. Your network, through the power of geometric progression, can reach out worldwide.

Let us say you have five key contacts and that they each have five key contacts and so on. This gives you access to 5 x 5 x 5 x 5 x 5 = 3,125 people. You can see the value of being "well networked" and how your "social capital" can be actually an asset. Of course it is not always the quantity of your contacts but the quality that matters. It definitely makes a difference if you have some "key influencers".

Unfortunately, what this means is that, at business or social events, people make a beeline for those who are perceived to be successful, either in monetary terms or in terms of their "clout". It works much better to be more relaxed and talk to everyone there. There is no point going if all you do is talk to the friends you came with. Ironically, the new people you meet, even if they are unlikely to present you directly with any business opportunity, will almost certainly know someone who will. People pick up quickly on insincerity or those who will only talk to perceived "heavyhitters".

Bad networking

One of the worst examples of networking I came across was in the USA. I was on an entrepreneurship course and an evening workshop was held to teach us how to network the American way. The networkers either told us their life story or very quickly left us when they realised we could not provide venture capital or whatever their most significant requirement was. The course leader was approached by a delegate, a medium-ranking development officer, whilst he was speaking to a senior-ranking aerospace delegate. As he shook hands, he actually looked away from the development officer and continued his conversation with the aerospace "heavyhitter". This is the type of networking that turns people off. You are there to meet people. If you do not show sincerity or respect for them, you will create the "negative networking syndrome". Bad news spreads twice as quickly as good news, as the story above illustrates.

How to network

Always aim to meet two new people in any networking event. It's natural after meeting new contacts to think, "How can I use them to move my career / business forward?" The "using" of people turns a lot of people off the concept of making new contacts. However, once you have met someone who you have found interesting, you should "keep in touch" and see whether there is any way you can be of assistance to them. If you take this attitude, you should be setting up a network of giving and receiving in an ethical way.

Be organised
The consequences of not being organised can counter the advantages of creating a strong network. You need to keep in touch with your network, otherwise it dies. Making contact is only "half the battle"; keeping in contact is very important. Set unambitious, but achievable, targets to keep in touch with your network.

Let me give you an example of how not to do it, again from my own repertoire. As a young ambitious consultant, I was busy making contacts, looking for referral business. One enterprise agency manager, in particular, sent me 40 new clients in the first six months, a godsend for my new business. I really liked him (quite apart from all the clients he sent me) and enjoyed spending time in his company. But, I became so busy that I never made time to see him for a whole year, feeling that having a cup of coffee with him was not "chargeable time". As a result, I lost touch with a person I liked and respected. Also, he stopped referring me business, not through any fall-out but, because we were not in touch regularly, when he came to the point of referring a client, I was no longer the first name to spring to mind. A salutary lesson for me.

Networking plan

You should aim to meet at least three new people a week in connection with your business. Your job then is to keep in touch with them on a planned basis.

For some of you, networking will come easily, others may already be blessed with a network through family contacts. However, whatever the state of your network, work at it.

The keys are:

1 Network on an ongoing basis.

2 Keep in touch regularly.

3 Try to help at least one person in your network every week.

Silverman, an American marketing guru, claims that networking is the number one marketing strategy for all companies. The reality is that, at times, your network may be the difference between success and failure in business.

You have to find the right balance and go about networking in a structured fashion. Set outcomes, review your performance at networking events, learn from great networkers. However, do it in a relaxed fashion. You are meeting new people and connecting. If you are too focused on an immediate business return, people will feel used and the benefits, both directly and indirectly, will be significantly lower. Be sincere and continually search for interesting ways to help and connect with your networks.

Let's network!

SELLING

The concept of selling, sadly, is an alien word to many people who want to be enterprising, start businesses or make projects happen. Most people see selling as some type of socially-unacceptable activity, where people are "sold" something they don't want or need by someone who "cons" them into buying the product or service. People spend their whole life avoiding this activity. However, this need not be the case. As Robert Louis Stevenson said, "Everyone is selling something all the time".

If selling means persuading someone to buy a product / service or idea, then everyone does it. Any form of selling activity should follow on from market research and promotional activity. Trying to persuade someone to buy something they don't want or need is a waste of time and very inefficient. However, even with a properly targeted audience, you will have to persuade people to buy or support your project. You will need to sell yourself to your prospective boyfriend / girlfriend, his / her parents, prospective employer and a bank manager for money. The list is endless. Persuasive communication is one of the key transferable skills you will need, wherever you work in life.

If you decide to work in the charitable sector, you will need to persuade potential sponsors to back you, persuade your chosen target group to use the charity and influence volunteers to commit time and effort to the project.

So my basic premise is that everyone needs to go on a sales course. It is just that we have all been programmed to hate that word. Don't mention the "S" word. It is ok to influence but not to sell.

I was attending a management development programme in London and was asked by one of the English participants what was my area of research and how I planned to apply the business model we were working on. I explained that I would be applying it to sales. Unfortunately, being of Northern Irish extraction, I pronounced my vowels rather differently to someone from England. My new friend thought I was working with "seals" and was therefore a zoo-keeper or circus-performer. The misunderstanding continued for three days, until he asked me whether I worked with any other animals! We eventually realised that we had been talking about different things. However, I sometimes believe that many people would rather work with "seals" rather than learn how to make "sales".

Learn the skills and use them appropriately and ethically. Much of what you achieve in life will be based on what deal you make with family friends and business associates. Until the other party agrees to back your proposal, nothing happens. Persuade and influence in an ethical way or leave everything to chance. It is your choice.

Selling is a process

There are stages that any sales or influence situation goes through. So let's analyse each stage as it happens and see what behaviours you need to adopt or learn.

Do your homework

It is important to ensure that you are talking to the right person. There's no point trying to do a deal with the person, unless that person can make the decision or at least is interested in talking to you. Do your market research and do not waste your time targeting the wrong audience for your product or service. For too long, the sales industry has worked on the principle of, "Sell your product to anyone you can find, whether they are interested or not" – no wonder selling has a bad name! Persevering is a strong quality but hounding people who do not want to know is unethical and wastes a lot of time.

Prospecting

"Qualify" your prospects – that means making sure they really *are* prospects. One of the key ways of ensuring that you only deal with people who are potentially interested in buying is to build a steady flow of prospects whom you can work with on a relaxed basis. You don't then have to "power-hose" the one or two people you have found by chance and you can concentrate on finding the right mix of person *versus* product or service to make the sale and achieve genuine lasting customer satisfaction.

How do you prospect?

Find out as much as possible about your potential customer. Let us say your ideal customer is a woman, aged 25-35, with a child under 5, and a family income of £35,000. Where do they live? What do they spend money on? Where do they shop? You need to develop a system to make these women aware of what you offer. You need to use a variety of low cost strategies to create enquiries.

Use six to seven different strategies. If they are targeted at an audience who clearly need the benefits of your products, this mix of strategies will put a number of enquiries into your pipeline. However, it is important to do this on an ongoing basis so that you never run out of potential customers or deals. What most people do, be it someone starting a business or someone looking to get potential members to their new club, is to stop prospecting the minute they think they have enough business or enquiries for their project. It is better to continually work at prospecting, because converting interest into sales or deals will vary and you will need to play a numbers game. A rule of thumb that sales people often follow is that you need 10 enquiries to get an appointment and 10 appointments to get a sale – that means you need to start with 100 enquiries to get one sale.

Relax, not everyone will buy

If there is one lesson you could learn from this chapter, it would be this: Not everyone will buy from you, even though market research has shown them to be an interested customer. Yet many of us are sensitive souls at heart. If we talk to someone about our project, and they do not give us a positive response, we take it personally.

I used to run a programme for women entrepreneurs. Many excellent graduates came on the course. They had good ideas, and worked hard at developing their business. Unfortunately, when most of them tried to make their first sale, and were not successful, they were devastated and a lot of their businesses did not go any further.

It's a national pasttime: "avoid selling".

Listen and ask questions

I have mentioned the importance of listening before but it is a key skill in persuading others. Listen to what they say and look for signs in their tonality or body language, which indicate what their key area of concern is. To get the right information, ask questions to get their reaction. Ask open questions that allow the potential customer to show their true motivation. You are trying to find out what their "hot button" is, what matters most to them and you are trying to diagnose whether you can provide a solution with your product / service.

The big moment, which tests your integrity, is when you have listened to the needs of the potential client and find that your business does not offer an appropriate solution to their needs. Are you prepared to walk away, even though you desperately need the sale? The answer is you have got to be ready to walk away. If you want to build a relationship of trust with the customer, you must act in their interests. Easy saying that, I know. But play fair today, get rich tomorrow!

The real answer lies in developing more prospects, and having people continually going through the "pipeline", so you can be more relaxed about who buys now.

Dealing with objections / closing

Welcome objections from potential customers who do not appear to want to buy – they give you the chance to deal with any potential problems.

You have also got to be prepared to close. A classic example of someone not doing this was John Cleese, when playing the part of a sale rep who was calling to a stationery shop, week after week, and having cups of tea with the owner. A stranger appeared one day, with forms to be signed, and then he left as soon as the forms were signed. John Cleese innocently asked, "Who is that?". "Oh", came the response, "that's the man we buy our stationery from". What was the message? John Cleese represented all those people who make contacts with potential prospects and succeed in building a relationship but never actually ask for business.

If you want to achieve results with your selling / presentations, you must ask for the work / business. It is a nice to think that once you have made contact with the "customer" that they will offer you the business. However, you need to ask for what you want. Sir Alan Sugar of "The Apprentice" fame is very clear in advising would-be entrepreneurs to ask clearly for what they want.

Part of the problem goes back to the fear of rejection. As part of the cultural bias against the concept of selling, some people will react rather inappropriately if they feel they are being sold to. You need to relax and realise that "some will, some won't", so what next? Asking for the sale, yet being relaxed about the outcome is the key.

Closes

Some professional sales people will learn a variety of closes in order to "trick" the customer into buying. You need to ask for the sale as part of the process and pick up on the signs where the customer still wants to buy and where he is wriggling out of a purchase.

Like every negotiation, the sale is only made when the contract is signed and money changes hands. It is vital to tie down the final details, because this can be the difference between actually getting the business or not.

Like all skills, you will get better at closing with practice. Selling and personal influence are very similar and, ultimately, you will be judged by the results you achieve. However, you may learn more from the sales or negotiations you lose than the ones you win. Take at least half an hour after every major "pitch" to assess what you did right or wrong. If you have been interviewed for a job, you have the right to ask for feedback. Gradually, you will get better. It is not always obvious what you have done wrong and you may need to rely on informal feedback and non-verbal signs.

A friend of mine, who was being interviewed for a job when he was a teenager, shut the door in the face of the second interviewer when walking nervously into the room. He didn't get the job (what a surprise!). It is not always obvious, but learn from your mistakes and you will get better.

AIDA

As said earlier, sales is a process. It is important that you do things in the right order: Attention; Interest; Desire; and Action. This is the normal process you need to stage manage before you have a chance to make the sale. Following this process will gradually build interest and lead to the opportunity for a decision. Let's see how it works.

A – Attention
Whether doing a presentation at a job interview or doing a "pitch", you need to get the attention of the people you are dealing with. Hopefully, if you have done your homework before the meeting, you will have an idea of the best way to attract the attention of your audience. What you are searching for is their "hot button", what will attract their attention. For instance, if you were trying to sell a product and you know the company's main focus is on cutting costs, an opening remark like, "This product will save you £15,000 per annum" is likely to get you a fair hearing.

I – Interest
You need to get your audience interested. Be clear and communicate in a meaningful way to attract and keep their interest. Do everything possible to bring your presentation alive, use visuals, vary your voice – if it's a product you are selling, have a sample. Make sure your communication style is appropriate for your audience. If you are trying to "sell" community service to teenagers, you need to talk their language and build rapport in your presentations. Again, being clear about what you want to achieve is necessary. Excellent communicators are flexible and will take notice if their audience are losing interest.

D – Desire
Basically, your audience will only want a solution if you can show that you can give them one of their main desires / benefits. By this stage, you should have found out what they are and you need to show how you can meet these

desires. Equally, if you can't genuinely meet at least one of their key desires / benefits, you should not pretend. Honesty at this stage will give you a strategic advantage with your potential customer in the long run.

A – Action
If you have got your potential client interested and have shown how you can solve their problems, the key now is to ask for the sale to see whether they are prepared to take action. If they say, "Let me think about it", that means they are not ready. It is important to read what the client is really thinking when they are looking for a way out, in order to avoid wasting your own time.

Flexibility

Ultimately, although you follow the same basic process, how you behave can depend on what you are selling and who you sell to. It is good to have a process and to organise each stage. However, each company / person you sell to is different and it is important that you respect that difference. Some will need help in making a decision, some will not respond to any kind of aggressive approach. Your ability to deal with a wide range of audiences will depend on your competencies, including belief, self-confidence and the ability to master your fears.

However, the most important thing is to change your own attitude to selling. It is a natural communication process and a vital life-skill. If you are to achieve goals, you must influence other people to support your cause; provided you do it with integrity, it can make the difference whether a business deal is done, a community project is backed by funders or, indeed, whether a relationship is formed.

You have been learning a wide range of enterprise skills. Basically, an entrepreneur finds an idea and makes it happen. To make your project happen, you will need to convince a lot of people, suppliers, customers, banks and staff to support you and to believe in your project. Your ability to influence them to support you will play a key role in the success or failure of the project. Influence or fail!

If you have very little of these skills and no network, you may feel you are not in a position to influence what happens. However, start where you are now, decide what decisions you need influence with, set a plan and if you complete the tasks set, gradually you will improve your ability to influence customers. You can do it, if you start practising the skills in everyday life. It's up to you!!

TASK 6.4

1 You have been asked to sell a new student health drink that cures hangovers. Prepare a three-minute pitch. Create a short written plan, then actually make the pitch to friends / family – ask for feedback.

2 Look ahead over the next three months to a situation where you will need to persuade someone to back you. Create a sales plan. Practise delivering it. Then carry out the actual presentation – what did you learn? What can you do better?

3 List 10 things you can improve to help your influencing skills.

4 Try to meet three new people every week who are important to your business.

5 Twice a week for the next month, find an opportunity to practice or to gain new skills.

6 A businessperson announces that they want to give £20,000 to the best sales pitch they receive this month. What idea would you send them? Why should they back you?

7 Practise persuasion skills every day.

7
LEADERSHIP & TEAMWORK

LEADERS

You need to be a leader. Whatever project you are involved in, you need to use all the resources available, including yourself, to make it happen. This will include buildings and finance but, above all, people. Leadership is not management. You need to inspire teams to achieve the projects and be the best you can be. Leadership is your capacity to turn a vision into reality.

Leadership traits

Leaders are congruent
To be a leader, you need to have several of the E-Factors in your behavioural make-up. You need to be able to take action, to know what your customers' needs are, to understand business issues, to have confidence and personal mastery, and the ability to influence others to follow your leadership and, as a team, to make the project happen.

You will be naturally better at some of the E-Factors than others but, if you want your team to be innovative, to develop personally and to learn, you need to set an example and show them that you are dedicated to the principles you are asking them to follow. In other words, "walk your talk". Are you paying lip service to the ideas of the new project or are you dedicated and prepared to work along with your team?

Belief
Part of your goal as a leader is to have belief in your vision. Not only do you have to deal with your own doubts, you must inspire others by the power of your belief to take action to achieve the vision. This belief should not waver, at least in public, until the project is achieved.

Vision

You should have a clear, strategic vision of where you want you and your team to end up. Can you see clearly the outcome of the project? Can you see it happening? Can you think strategically beyond where you are now?

How do you get better at this? Practise visualising long-term goals and the strategic aims of your organisation.

Team player

Ironically, most of the time as a leader, you need to be a team player. You may need to lead the team but you also need to be integrated with it and be able to work within the dynamics of the business, using the power of the team to realise your objectives.

Inspire

You must inspire others to join your team, your company and to take action. Your belief will do that but you also need to motivate others, and to give them belief that the project will happen. The ability to "sell" them on your business or company is significant.

Flexible

Flexibility is one of the key qualities of the enterpriser. You need to know when to inspire, when to allow the team to get on with it, and when you must intervene to deal with a major blockage. Although most theorists would now favour a team-based leadership approach, your style of leadership may need to vary according to the type of organisation you are leading, the type of project and the type of people involved. Many leaders tend to have one style that works for them about 70% of the time. Can you vary your style when a situation, or the people involved, require something different?

Leadership is very much a communication process and thus you need to follow the standard communication process discussed earlier:

- Know what you want: If you, as leader, do not know where you want to end up, what chance does anyone else have?

- Take action and be able to measure whether you are getting the outcome you need at this stage.

- The ability then to change strategy if the first strategy is not working is the mark of the good leader who knows that goals are not always achieved in a stereotypical way.

Delegate
As a leader, although it is good to have an idea of what happens with the detail, you cannot afford to get bogged down in day-to-day details. Leaders need to find others to deal with these, while they focus on taking the business or company forward.

Face the 20% that cause the problems
In running any business project, there are many things to do. However, there are certain key issues that are always likely to cause problems – for instance, confrontations with troublemakers or difficult decisions that need to be made. You shouldn't delegate these, they are the responsibility of the leader! It is these key activities that will make a difference and are where a leader will make their mark.

The ability to think perceptually
When you are making decisions regarding the future of your company, it is important to be able to see customer, staff and other stakeholder viewpoints, as well as your own. The ability to gauge any changes in these other viewpoints is a responsibility of the leader.

Break things down
As well as sharing the vision, you need to be involved in the design of the shorter steps that will take you there and in overcoming the obstacles that might get in your way.

Find managers who are better than you
If you are recruiting a team to take the business forward, look for people with special abilities. You may feel threatened by them initially but you need their expertise. Even if you are a small business start-up, with all the lack of resources that implies, look for key staff or external advisers who have the capacity to help you realise your vision. Using someone who is cheaper tends to be short-term thinking.

Look for communications opportunities
Find new and creative ways to make things happen.

Rewards / compensations
Give people a vested interest in the business to lock them in for the long-term. Use short-term celebrations as opportunities to reward people and to show your appreciation in an unexpected way.

Clear up the leadership / management distribution
It is your job to create values and to design how the plan is going to work. You will need the help of management to execute. You also should make the key decisions, once you have sought expert advice. Your auditors or business consultants may give sound advice as to how to run the business but you, as leader, must decide and use them to help you make your decision which is the one that matters.

Everything you do matters
As a leader, you set the organisational culture. If you come in late, or don't carry out promises or threats, people at all levels of the organisation will act the same. I have worked for organisations where the leader was very negatively into micromanagement and tended to have similar people in positions of control. Needless to say, that was not a very motivating environment. I have also worked for organisations where the leader had a vision that inspired all the staff and made you want to be part of the team that brought about the impossible.

Tough but fair
I fully support the collaborative leadership model, where achievements are very much the team effort. However, there is a human trait where, if you appear too "nice", people that they feel they can "push their luck". If you have good information and communication systems, you will hear through the "grapevine" where someone is doing this, possibly carrying out activities that conflict with your mission. The danger, of course, is in overreacting to small issues. However, rest assured, if one of your managers has done something that you don't approve of, it will quickly become a habit they will not stop, and you can end up with a much more significant problem.

Leaders are listeners / readers
You should always be looking for information, formal and informal, and listening to feedback, both external and internal.

Leaders are creative
Your ability to solve strategic problems creatively is important, together with your reaction to the fast pace of innovation. You should be open to new ways of doing things because, if you find the right innovation, you may be able to change things significantly for your business.

Leaders like to learn
I am constantly amazed by the leaders of growing and large companies, who are keen to learn, to build clusters and to network with other chief executives. They may have achieved conventional success but they are constantly looking for one or two ideas, often from competing industries, that will make a difference in their own particular business.

Coaching
I see coaching from two angles. First, as a leader, you should be able to coach others to motivate them and to provide the springboard for them to achieve high performance. Your job is to listen and facilitate the development of your key objectives.

However, who coaches the coach? As a leader, you may be in a position where, although there may be boards of directors or shareholders to whom you report, there is no one acting as your mentor or coach to guide you through the challenges you face. You need someone not involved in the day-to-day decisions of your business to help facilitate you in your decision-making. Getting coaching is a worthwhile investment in yourself. You set out your goals and have someone as a sounding board to motivate, encourage and help you, without being directly involved in your career.

Respect other people's style
You should have the capacity to work with a variety of senior people with different styles. You need to work on your ability to create rapport with them all, and your capacity to create group rapport when you all meet together.

Trust
Creating a climate of trust and integrity is your job. You need to gain the trust and respect of your team rather than get it only because of your position. How you behave ultimately decides whether your team trusts you and will work with you.

TASK 7.1

Are you a leader? What is your vision of your organisation's future?

Learn from models
There are many people who have successfully created a transformation of organisations, large and small, private and public. Read their books, network with them, watch what they do. Copy their behaviour that works.

Values
It is up to you to impose the values of your organisation from the top. Those values might include things such as customer service or integrity. You need to set them out so that it is very clear that this is how everyone must act.

Your personal leadership style
Are you clear what your personal leadership style is? How can you enrich it? How can you improve it? You should be looking to acquire behavioural skills that will achieve the results of good leadership. Identify any weaknesses in your style. Can you unblock any competencies where you have been found wanting?

TASK 7.2

Suppose you have developed from being a successful small business owner into a senior leader in a public sector organisation. How would you have adapted your behaviour to be the best leader you can be in that particular situation?

Confidence
As a leader, you need to be confident and well-organised. You may not always feel confident about yourself or your business. However, your influence on all the stakeholders is important. Your confidence will be infectious but so also will be any obvious lack of confidence. Your style will influence what the organisation does.

How do you motivate your team?
You must make people feel part of a team, offer them opportunity for advancement and to fulfil their ambitions within your organisation. To do so,

you need to take time to listen to key individuals and to watch their non-verbal language, together with their words, to assess what is really important to them.

State management
Your ability to control your state and focus (see *Personal Mastery* below) is important, as in times of crisis your team will look to you for the way forward. Your ability to appear calm, focused and in a powerful state will have a strong impact on how the organisation as a whole responds.

The ability to give your best performance, when you want it, is important. The challenge you may have is that you may only work at your best when under stress, so you need to be able to recreate this state at any time not just in a fire-fighting crisis. The better your performance as leader at the strategic stage, the less fire fighting there will be.

Use planning and creative models
Part of your job is to plan the future of your organisation. You need to have the capacity to see creative possibilities, to allow others or yourself to suggest new ideas and then to be able to disassociate yourself and to take a critical view in order to iron out any practical difficulties.

Overcome limiting beliefs
A key challenge will be to overcome the limiting beliefs of other key influencers in your organisation. You need to understand their perspective, respect it and find a way to win them to your way of thinking. This may include achieving small targets, building trust and belief step-by-step.

The right message
I have shown what an important part communication plays in leadership. The worry is that other key players may get the wrong message. Miscommunication can be very difficult. You need to consider carefully the media you use, to ensure that it is appropriate to achieve the clarity that is needed. Communication and persuasion will play an important part in your leadership style.

Learning
Your ability to lead the group is influenced by your own beliefs and functions. Being aware of this is half the battle. You also need to learn the demands of

your particular leadership situation. Sometimes, you will need your team to develop all the ideas; sometimes, you will need to do a lot of stimulation.

Leadership skills

Research has revealed a lot of skills you can develop. It is not enough to know you should show strong belief. This is a behaviour / skill that you must work on to take it to the level of unconscious competence, where, through practice, you appear to be a born leader.

The skills of a leader can be divided up as follows.

Personal mastery

1   Establish a vision and a set of interim steps to implement that vision.
2   Keep yourself, your goals and personal states aligned to your mission.
3   Practice building your belief to achieve your mission.
4   Work on your flexibility in leadership style and ability to influence skills.

Working with others

Realise that people do think differently. You need to win over people who are against the changes you want to achieve and you need to overcome their resistance to change by whatever methods work best in that situation. Your respect, your ability to listen, your ability to build rapport and your ability to put yourself in the position of those against the changes are a good start, before you begin your campaign of influencing. Look at how styles work with people, the problems and the level of change.

Skills requirement

You need to be able to motivate and communicate to your highest level. You will need to work, at times, not only on your own tasks but on those people you need to influence. Unless you match your mission with their values, or get them to change their values, you will face a strong resistance to change.

Sporting heroes

Some of you love sport and some of you have no interest in it. However, sporting leaders do behave in many of the ways outlined and can be great role models. When Liverpool were losing 3-0 at half-time in the final of the Champions League to AC Milan, the hot favourites, somehow Stephen

Gerrard, the captain, and Rafael Benitez, the manager, turned things around. Benitez was very calm at half-time. He did not speak of victory, but of getting a goal back, a first step, and he changed the players' tactics as clearly the initial strategy was not working. He also reminded the players to play their best to show their appreciation to the fans, all 42,000 of them who had turned up at Istanbul and were singing the Liverpool anthem, "You'll never walk alone", even after watching their team being humiliated in the first half. Benitez then set the team a short-term goal of scoring in the first 10 minutes of the second half. When Gerrard, their leader on the pitch, responded with a fantastic goal, he motivated the rest of the team that they could do more. The rest is history. A wonderful example of belief, flexibility, action and leadership, linked to great teamwork.

There are lots of examples of political leaders, locally and abroad, who have worked to a mission and made substantial progress in its achievement. However, I think I will stay clear from naming examples – this book is controversial enough!

I also do believe that as well wanting to win, you need to finish the job. In another sign of leadership, Benitez, the Liverpool manager, got rid of some of his squad who, although they over-performed in the final, did not "do the business" on a consistent basis. This may seem ruthless but, for a project to develop, you will have to make tough decisions that will work strategically but may often be very unpopular in the short-term. Some people find this impossible, particularly if they have excellent rapport with their existing team. People need to be treated properly but the mission is everything and sacrifices have to be made. There are even examples of leaders who have removed themselves personally from the chief executive role for the good of the organisation. Many entrepreneurs who have the leadership qualities to take a business from nothing to the growth stages may well want to leave the "stage" at plc stage when the company is listed on the stock market, as they realise they are inappropriate leaders for a company in this environment where relations with "the City" and corporate governance regulations become much more significant.

Ethics
If the leader's ethics are suspect, this can lead to a lack of ethics at all levels of the organisation. The ethical mindset of the leader should cascade down through an organisation. Just think of Enron!

Clear communication
Everyone you deal with should be clear what you expect of them.

Promote learning
You should encourage all staff to develop to be the best they can be. For some, this may be scary, a bit like bringing in highly talented individuals whose abilities you feel may surpass your own. However, bringing people in and looking for peak performance should be a value that sets your organisation apart.

Decision-making
When the time comes, you will have to make difficult decisions. How do you get good at decision-making? Probably by making bad decisions and learning from them. An appreciation of all the key business dynamics, including marketing, finance and people, is important, as sometimes a leader who is a specialist in one of these areas will tend to make a decision that focuses on the comfort zone of their own discipline. For instance, a leader with a marketing background might overlook strategic financial or people consequences in their decision, focusing only on the marketing aspects with which he / she is comfortable.

Energy
You need to have the energy to manage change and keep a project moving on. Hopefully, you will have something left for your private life in order to maintain a work / life balance. The ability to relax, no matter what the circumstances, is good, not only so you can make detached and unemotional decisions in times of crisis, but also because too much stress saps your energy and undermines your capacity to perform. Time spent with family or taking exercise will tend to be time well spent, even from the business perspective.

However, driving a project ahead in uncertain conditions can create an adrenalin rush that can be addictive. However, when you see high performers taking time off on a regular basis, you may realise that energy, relaxation, exercise and an outside life can be much better not only for you but also the business. Beware of being "busy" doing things that don't really make a difference to the end result. An hour wasted at the office is an hour you could have spent with your loved ones, or just enjoying life.

Risk-taking decisions
One of the key lessons in this book is that you must be a risk-taker to be a successful entrepreneur. Even in the public sector, when you are put in charge of a new organisation, such as a new agency or programme, you are taking a risk to some degree. There is some truth in this but not in the "gung-ho" sense of a kamikaze pilot who dives in, not caring what the consequences are for anyone, including him or herself. Any new enterprise is a step into uncertainty. The best business plan in the world cannot guarantee what is going to happen and, even with the best-laid plans, you may have to change direction and to use all your innovative skills to respond and keep the organisation going.

What separates the entrepreneur starting up a small business from the manager of a new company subsidiary in a large organisation are the more serious implications for the individual if the venture fails. Most small ventures are started with inadequate resources, just small amounts of capital from the funder. The owner is personally liable for debts, unless he operates under the protection of limited company status but, even with that protection, he / she is likely to lose more financially than the corporate new venture manager, who at worst will lose their job and possibly a bonus but, provided the failure is not linked directly to their inadequacies, may be moved to a different role within the company.

So, yes, a leader is a risk-taker, because they will often be instigating change and pursuing a strategic vision in an uncertain environment. However, even the entrepreneur can – and should – limit their risk to a calculated level. The problem with your own venture is that you are allowed to take all the decisions, no matter what your previous experience, and often you lose the power of detachment. Your business can become an emotional attachment to which many people hold past its sell-by date for ego or because they want to keep the business going for staff or the community, even though the model no longer works.

So, yes, you do need to be a risk-taker, though the type and extent of the risk varies from project to project. The better you plan and use the E-Factor skills, the better your chance of success.

A good leader knows when to go

A great skill lies in knowing when to follow Kenny Rogers' advice in the song "The Gambler", "You got to know when to hold them, know when to fold them". Military leaders from time immemorial, when they sensed the battle was not going their way, knew when to cut their losses to live to fight another day.

Decisions under uncertainty

Managers can make decisions within definite operational structures. As a leader operating under uncertainty, you will have to develop the capacity to make decisions that are against popular opinion but that strategically make sense. You need to see possibilities that others don't see. You need to make decisions and be prepared to put a plan into action straight away.

Learn from your mistakes

Sometimes you will call it wrong. A leader will take responsibility and be prepared to learn from the failure. A leader knows that failure will happen, and will learn and, if need be, will change strategy or timescale to achieve the goal.

Ultimately, the hardest part of being a leader is to manage yourself so you carry out your inspirational role. Sometimes, you may feel as down as your team, but you have to have to hide it from them. Acting as if you believe will help, but always be yourself.

When I first went into business, I had a set vision that a leader had to be loud, a great public speaker who aggressively motivated the team. Having since observed many leaders, I notice there is a variety of styles. Some leaders will be quietly-spoken, supporting their key players and leading mainly by example. They are persuasive and lead by bringing the team along and only take a different approach when there is a need for a change of strategy.

As the leader, you set the agenda. You also set the culture of your organisation – whatever behaviour you expect your team to show, you must demonstrate yourself on an ongoing basis.

Although there are eight E-Factors in total, being enterprising involves identifying an innovation or opportunity and making it happen through your leadership skills. Sometimes, there will not be a large team within the company, but even one-person projects may involve working with regional agencies, suppliers, customers, banks and business advisers. Your ability to lead them and make them all work towards the mission will make the project happen. Develop your own leadership style. Your main example may be someone who has operated in a different time, company or project. Learn from others but develop your own style, based on your beliefs and strengths. Someone who can lead others need not have any particular technical knowledge but they must have the capacity to develop strategic vision and make it happen. Find opportunities to lead. Your ultimate potential will be realised when you develop as a leader, create a new project and make it happen with a team. After that, anything is possible.

TASK 7.3

In the next month, find at least one opportunity to lead a project in business or the community. Make it a project that you are passionate about. Make it happen, learn along the way and, above all, have fun!

TEAMS

You will have noticed that, in this chapter, I write about both leadership and teams. In my view, the two areas are linked. A team needs to be led and a leader will get his vision realised only through an excellent team. Many people who go into entrepreneurship start off with the concept of doing it alone. However, any enterprise will benefit from group work and from the synergy that a good team can provide.

Team development

Any team will take time to develop. There will be possible conflict, as everyone finds their roles at the start and the team will go through a process of development, storming, norming and performing. That is why a clever leader needs to be there to coach, to facilitate and to cajole as the team performs.

One of the problems is that, sometimes, you will have someone on a team who does not want to be there. They should be given every chance to get into alignment with all other members of the team; however, if this fails, sometimes you have to consider an exit route, if they are not adding value to the team.

There is room for different roles
Management development research has revealed that the ideal team has a mix of individuals all with different strengths. Intuitively, the ideal would appear to have everyone with very similar outlooks and skills but, in practice, a mix of skills and outlooks has been shown to perform much better, provided they can work as a team. Most teams need a leader-facilitator, a strong team player who will always focus on team-togetherness, someone to raise alternative viewpoints and someone to persuade people to take action. Not only must all these individuals bring their own individual skills to the team, they must also respect the team and want it to perform well. Whatever its healthy differences, the team all should have the same mission, with a compelling reason why they are together.

The purpose
Just as it is important for you to have a purpose, a group / team also needs one. A purpose is particularly vital at the early stage, when there is some

inevitable conflict, and also again at a later stage, when a lot of the hard work has been done and perhaps the group cannot quite finish off the project.

"Why are you here?" is the key question. In many cases, the "why" is more compelling than the "how". I suggest that you get your team together as early as possible and insist that everyone has to answer the question, "Why am I here?". The group, no doubt, will have conflicting purposes and ideas but you need to find a common purpose. Until the purpose of the project matches that of the group, negativity will be encouraged. It would be good if the group could get inspired or motivated at this stage; however, grandiose motivational speeches have their place, but their effect too easily can wear off.

At this stage, too, the team needs to create its values, and to set a blueprint as to how it will achieve the strategic goal.

A facilitator can be useful in resolving conflicts and driving the purpose agenda. The facilitator also can help to build the vision, to work on beliefs and to challenge any negative beliefs that start to surface.

Develop
Everyone in the team should have an agreed personal development plan (PDP). Team activities should be arranged to encourage team-building. Everyone should understand roles other than their own. The use of reward and recognition to show that the team appreciates each individual will help also.

Team power

Although you may be the leader of the project, you should use the power of the team. You should seek opportunities to allow others to show leadership. A series of team tasks will help to make the team believe they can get results together and will build a sense of morale – always be looking for the team and individuals to stretch a little further each time.

Be positive
Look to reward and to recognise anyone who is acting for the good of the team or who is actively developing new behaviours.

Have fun: a team that plays together, works together. This should not be forced, but a systematic series of fun events will change the team's make-up.

I worked in one organisation, where we all mainly worked as consultants on individual projects. When we had fun days or evenings out, every event seemed to create a potential team spirit. The only problem was that there was a year between each event and, in between, we all went back to our own individual projects. Ironically, although most of us have now left the organisation, we still get on well. What a waste of group potential that was.

TASK 7.4

Think of a team project you were involved in. How did the team function? What role did you play? Was this the most suitable role for you?

Are you a team player or a loner?

Many of you will start your own organisation because you want to run things your way. However, you will need other people to help you. When you start, you might be responsible for operations, HR, marketing and accounts – simply because you cannot afford to hire specific people to take on these roles. But, as you expand your business, you must build a team over these specific functions.

You will find this difficult, particularly if you have ignored the value of being a team-player from the start. However, much of the enterprise literature shows that the creation and building of a team and a team ethos within a company plays a strong role in the company's success. Some of the most effective teambuilding activity I have seen done by entrepreneurs is where they manage to turn their bank manager, accountant, lawyer and business advisers into an informal, but seamless, team that works together on each project. You may have initiated the project but can you listen to others and get the benefits of team synergy – and energy? Can you take on board the input of others or will you bulldoze them down? Big business is a team sport and you must learn these team skills.

People skills

Can you give feedback to other team members? Can you motivate and encourage them for the good of the team? Can you show and give trust and build rapport with other team members? A genuine interest in understanding the perspective of others is important. Honesty is vital but you need diplomacy, particularly in the early stages, to know how far you can go.

Group brainstorming
As soon as you can get together a group of people from diverse backgrounds, ask them to come up with ideas for a new project. Prepare to be surprised how a group can come together and how their different perspectives can lead to the creation of a wide variety of ideas.

Have a team coach
It is useful to have someone not directly involved in the team to facilitate the group. Observation of how people perform in a group, with individual feedback, can help people adjust their behaviour. In many groups, the key problem is someone who naturally dominates the group. This can demotivate other members from taking part. Hopefully, the group will bring them into line but, at an early stage, a facilitator might help to prevent problems.

TASK 7.5

Have a group meeting you attend videoed. Get someone to observe and let the group watch the video. Who is open to learning?

Entrepreneurs may be used to working on their own but must learn to respect the group and realise that their behaviour must adapt in a group.

Original individuals
Many people who normally do not contribute much individually, in the right group dynamic can make an effective contribution. It is all about getting to the Three Musketeers' "one for all, all for one" attitude. People want to be valued and want to play their part.

I was recently involved in presenting an enterprise course. Students were assigned randomly to a group, which had to complete a number of tasks over the period of a week. My role was to facilitate the group. The group had everything: a very difficult individual who did not share the values of the rest of the group, a very strong-minded dominant individual, as well some people lacking in confidence. My role was not to tell the group what to do but, at times, to ask questions to help self-awareness. The group went through some very difficult patches early on, particularly in regard to consensus decision-making. Gradually, the group took shape, and the difficult individual and the dominant one both became more team-players. Again, it followed the standard procedure of storm / norm / perform. The group found its own way to work. They were helped by having to complete a number of group tasks designed by the Belbin group, where physical tasks could only be completed by teamwork.

Belbin

Cambridge professor Meredith Belbin has developed interesting psychometric tests to help provide information on how you perform in a group. What do you like to do in any team situation? The challenge often is that, if you have a number of excellent individuals who all want to lead, there is likely to be conflict until a team consensus on leadership is found. An excellent lesson from the course above was how important it is to be a team-player. Many would-be entrepreneurs need to take time to understand this concept. Equally, the group has to guard against assuming the qualities of an ineffective committee. The group needs to find someone who will keep them on course, and not let it descend into a talking-shop, without serving its goals or mission.

TASK 7.6

Set up a small team to generate business ideas. Meet once a month for three months. Work to build a team. What did you learn? Would you have had more ideas as an individual?

The ski trip

It does take time to form a group. Many entrepreneurs keep bringing people in to the business and then replace them immediately, trying to find the right person to fit the needs of the business - instantly. The ideal is to give a new team a sense of achievable tasks and, as momentum builds up, to really go for it.

On a recent ski trip, I was able to observe and learn a lot about group activity. We were a variety of school parents, thrown together for the trip. We were all beginners and all lacked confidence. As we went through the difficult early stages of learning to move on skis and then to tackle the more daunting tasks, the ski activity was full of lessons for teamwork. Some of us, who were falling less than others, initially became impatient with those who were taking longer to learn the basic skills. One admittedly quite fit individual, so highly did he rate his performance, moved himself up a group to intermediate after the first day. We did not miss his arrogant attitude towards the less talented skiers.

As well as learning individual ski skills, the instructor focused on developing us as a group for a specific reason. Eventually, we would be going into tougher conditions in uncertain weather and he knew that, if anything went wrong, we would need to stick together as a group. However, he did take it to extremes. As I lost control of my skis and was heading down the slope out of control, he advised, "Stay with the group, David". Everyone thought it was hilarious and needless to say I got the lesson. Gary, who was a bit of a daredevil and kept heading off in an opposite direction to the group, was asked constantly, "Where are you going, Gary?". I had great difficulty with the ski-lifts, particularly with the two main ones where you and your partner needed to stay balanced to keep it moving. However, at the end of the week, as a group, we all completed the ladies Olympic downhill. Those of us who were trying to excel individually had learnt that supporting the group and having respect for everyone, whatever their athletic ability, was more important than our own ego. The beer was good too! More team-building!

Conclusion

You need to learn to lead enterprises but also be a team-player. In fact, you need to learn to be a team-player in order to lead enterprises! This word "team" applies not only to colleagues within your company, but to external stakeholders. Collaborative relationships ultimately will prove much more successful, if you have a "win-win" approach. Learn to be a team player, lead from the front and watch that project happen!

TASK 7.7

List the teams you work with. List three things you can do to build the team / collaborative framework.

8

ACTION & RESULTS

You need to be outcome-orientated, that is to know constantly what you are looking for strategically, as well as in the here and now. However, without the capability to take action on an ongoing basis, you are unlikely to achieve any of your outcomes. Outcome / action orientation is a key enterprise competency and needs to be backed up by flexible behavioural patterns. Once you know what you want, you need to take action. However, there are likely to be changes or reactions that may get in the way of you achieving your targets. Your ability to notice feedback, verbal, written and more informal methods that tell you what result you are getting is key. If you are not getting the result required, you may need to adopt a different strategy, until you get the results you need.

This may seem obvious but, in the enterprise world, you often find individuals who push very hard but get mediocre results at best because they do not observe the above rules. These are often people who, when they have an idea in their heads, go for it immediately and take action without any thought to consequences or regarding what they really want. This is better sometimes than no action at all, but it is almost a "scattergun" approach – one step forward and then one step back. You also get individuals who, once they have devised a strategy, act on it and keep on doing so, regardless of the consequences – the effect is a bit like keeping banging your head on a wall hoping it will break. I know it may depend on how hard your head is and how soft the wall, but the fact remains that this is probably not a very effective approach.

Why do they do this? Well, if you are a disciple of positive thinking, you will have developed a Churchillian response, "Never give up – never ever give up". Determination and persistence are certainly valued qualities in someone starting an enterprise and rightly so. However, there may be a need to vary the strategy when it is not producing the results you expected.

Sometimes, you also may need to review your outcomes when something changes in your business model or the environment, which means that the original outcome is no longer valid. However, outcome orientation is being clear about what you want at both macro and micro levels. If you are unclear as to what you want and where you are going, the environment will reflect back your uncertainty and produce mixed results.

KNOW WHAT YOU WANT

What do you want? Or as The Spice Girls said (sorry!), "Tell me what you want, what you really really want". It is not always easy to know what you want, particularly at a strategic level. You can get too busy passing exams, making a living and just getting by. Even worse, you can often go into careers, relationships or even business agreements that are really based on someone else's wish-list. A friend may ask you to go into business with him / her or your father may have always wanted to be a doctor and, because he didn't achieve it, now wishes the same for you. You should not go for either option, unless it suits you. You can be vulnerable to other people's ideas, if you do not know what you want. Either have your own plan or resign yourself to being part of someone else's (not very enterprising!).

How do you know what you want?
You need to take some time out. It is good to start off with some "possibility thinking". If there were no limits, what would you like to do, how much money would you like to earn, what contribution would you want to make? Assume you have no limits.

TASK 8.1

Take five minutes and write down, as fast as you can, without stopping, everything you want to do or have in the next five years.

TASK 8.2

Look at your list from the task above. Pick one long-term and one short-term goal. How much do you want them? Why do you want them? Write these goals out once a day.

The most vital skill

You can see that knowing what you want is not as straightforward as you think, yet it is vital because you are setting out the direction of your life. Knowing where you are going and being able to measure it is critical. There is very little limit to what you can achieve, provided you have absolute clarity as to what you want. It is important that you know where you want to end up long-term, as well as short-term, to make sure you are on the right path. Many goal-setting specialists suggest thinking about where you want to be in 10 years' time. If you can visualise this, then work back to today to see the steps you must take in between. Try it now.

Your purpose

Life can change at any time. Your goals may vary but it may useful to have a mission statement, which sets out clearly what you want to do to contribute to making a difference. This may sound a little prosaic, but it is no more than accepting that you have a purpose to use your talents and abilities to help others. It is something to come back to if you are ever sidetracked, which can easily happen. Your purpose will usually include doing what you love and what you are good at – if possible, try to put your mission statement into one sentence. For example, let's say you enjoy coaching businesspeople, advising and encouraging them to be successful. Your mission statement could be, "I want to inspire and motivate businesspeople to perform at their best". Then, if that's your mission, everything you do in life should be related to achieving it.

The why

It is important that your mission really motivates you and gives you a reason for taking action. You should be passionate about it, otherwise it is not your mission. You may be familiar with company mission statements, often framed and sitting in the reception area of a major company. The problem is that these are often someone else's mission that you may not agree with.

Setting out your purpose

Name two of your talents. What are you good at and also really enjoy?

Suppose you are an excellent teacher and you are very enthusiastic. How do you enjoy using these skills? When have you used these qualities?

Suppose you have been the most enthusiastic when you have been teaching young children how to play tennis. They loved your approach, were making progress and really enjoying your lesson. It seems obvious that your purpose should be to teach tennis to kids. What we don't know is whether there are other areas you would like to share with people. My suggestion is that your mission statement should include sports coaching but perhaps go wider to include the general role of teaching. For example, "My mission is to teach others to be the best they can be, using my enthusiasm and people skills. I teach businesspeople and sportspeople of all ages to reach their potential and have fun".

This statement makes clear why you are here, what you are good at. You may use various ways to harness that talent to help others but everything you do should be geared to teaching and working with people, as it is clear that is what you love and what you are good at. When your purpose has these two qualities, it is much more likely that you will stick at it and make a bigger contribution.

What do you want to be?

Once you have sorted out the broad principle, it is now time to be more specific. You will need courage to state this, because it will seem as if the world makes decisions as to what you should do. Parents, friends, workmates, all will have pigeonholes they want to slot you in, perhaps partly for your own good (in their eyes) but also to achieve some goal of their own, sometimes one they are not consciously aware of.

Work on your want list again
Spend another 10 minutes writing down everything you want. You might start off with a list of material possessions such as a castle, a Maserati, etc. but, somewhere in the list, you may show what is important to you, what contribution you would like to make. For instance, let us say that when you go through your list, you find that sports is everything to you. It is the environment you want to be around. A careers adviser would probably say, "Fine, that's your hobby. Now what work can you do to pay for that hobby?". However, if you want to work in sports and you are unlikely to become a professional athlete, there are lots of other options available – for example, a sports agent, a sports coach, a sports lawyer, a physio, a sports finance person, working in or managing a leisure and sports complex, a sports journalist, developing new products for use in your favourite sport, selling sporting autographs and memorabilia, a sports psychologist. See how you can link your skills and enthusiasms to the area you love.

Where are you now?
People often find it hard to realise where they are now compared to their end vision. It is important to self-assess and, if need be, to get feedback from those around you. Don't fool yourself, there is no other place you can start from than where you are now.

Your vision

Try to build a picture of your future. Visualise your job, career or business. What is your income? What type of people do you work with? What exercise do you take? The bigger the vision, the more you will believe it.

Spend 10 minutes everyday going through that vision in the same detail.

It is important to know strategically what you want because, if you don't know where you are going in the long run, it is very easy to go off course. As

Tony Robbins, a renowned motivational speaker put it, "In ten years' time, you may not know what you want, but you will surely arrive!". It can seem like a waste of time to think 10 years ahead when today is so uncertain but, as Robbins says, while you are making up your mind about where you want to end up, you can wake up and realise 10 years have passed. It happens to too many people – don't let it happen to you!

Strategic goals can change but it is likely that your life purpose will always be with you. You may demonstrate or use it with different groups or situations, but the true essential you and your talents always will be there. This is important when drawing up your long-term vision as to where your talents will take you. For instance, a teacher who wants to share his / her subject with the world and be a successful business person may think, "That is not how education works, education is done within the public sector; a high level principal or administrative post must be my aim". However, look at the vision of Robert Kiyosaki, founder of the "Rich Dad / Poor Dad" brand, which teaches financial literacy. Robert is a teacher at heart but has created an online community that plays a game he uses to teach the principles of financial literacy. He also has a variety of information products that educate and conducts seminar tours, simply because he refused to limit his vision.

The power of goal-setting
You have read many times about the power of goal-setting. Basically, if you have goals, they tend to give you more direction and a greater chance of success. You need a list of goals, short-term and long term, for most aspects of your life. For instance, if your only goal was to have your own business by age 35, earning £150,000 per year, the danger is that, if that is all you focus on, it may be the only thing you achieve and you may find yourself with no personal or social life as a consequence, simply because you did not set goals in these areas. This example pleases the army of negative thinkers who use the lonely success story as an example of why it is better not to have goals. However, where goal-setters set targets in both their business and personal life, they can have success but not at any price, and a proper work / life balance.

Do you need to pay a price?
Depending on your goal, there usually is a price to pay. But I don't believe it has to be your social or family life. However, you do have to remove a lot of things from your life that do conflict with your goals – for example, you need

to make sure not to take on too many outside projects that could conflict with your aim. However, the power of goals lies in setting out targets that can measure your progress on the road to achieving your vision / life purpose.

Features and goals
Goals should be positive, specific and measurable. For instance, if you say, "I would like to give up smoking in the near future", you are not following a couple of these conditions.

First, your goal is negative. Second, there is no specific timescale set to target the outcome. This is not a goal, just a vague aim which, of course, is going to be much more difficult to achieve.

What will I see, hear and feel to know I have achieved my goal?
This is looking for the sensory evidence that will tell you that you have achieved what you set out to achieve.

What will I lose?
It is important to consider what benefits you are getting from the behaviour you want to change. When you are setting goals, it can be useful to question why you want it. For instance, you say you want a 7 series BMW, a good question to ask yourself would be, "Why do I want it". You may genuinely love German cars and really want this model but, if you find, as you might, that what you really want is to be respected and admired because you drive a 7 series BMW, then it is the feeling you want more than the actual item and it might be better to work on getting that feeling met in some other way.

Write your goals in detail
Spell out the detail of each goal, as this is important for visualisation, for your subconscious mind to accept it and start finding opportunities to make things happen.

Level of goals
You need goals that will stretch you but are still achievable. If your main goal is to have lunch in a restaurant two days this month, this is very achievable but will not stretch you at all. However, if you want to become President of the USA by Friday, that is pushing things too far. However, one of the key benefits of setting a goal, and then working towards it, is your personal development and what you will learn on your journey towards achieving it.

Key goal
What one goal could have an impact on all aspects of your life? Which goal would be life-changing?

Goal-setting should not be a one-off thing. It is something you do for the rest of your life. You should certainly have more than one goal.

Obstacles

You will find obstacles in the path of achieving your goals. In fact, someone once said that "Obstacles are what you see when you take your eye off your goal". Some obstacles lie within yourself, such as a specific fear; other obstacles provided by the outside world. It's useful to anticipate and plan for them – and even to welcome them as part of your own personal development. Obstacles are part of the goal achievement process and you must deal with them on your way to achieving your targets. Therefore, ideally, you want to find out as soon as possible what they are, and face them.

As noted, not only do you want to achieve your goals, but you should ask yourself, "What type of person do I have to become to achieve that goal?". That is why people who achieve against obstacles and have to stretch to achieve a goal have a greater advantage over someone who achieves the same goal by luck. If you become a millionaire by your own business and financial strategies, you will have developed a skill-set that you can turn to again and again; whereas, if you become a millionaire by wining the lottery, ironically it is another lottery as to whether you will hold on to the money and prosper, as your new wealth is not a result of a process of actions and skill development.

One step at a time
How do you eat an elephant? One bite at a time.

Once you have set your goals (I recommend 5-year, 1-year, quarterly, weekly and daily goals), it is the actions you carry out that will achieve the results – sometimes there will be an opportunity to have one significant breakthrough but usually goals are achieved step-by-step.

What resources do you have?
It is useful to identify what resources are needed to achieve the goals and whether you have these available to you now. Do you know the right people?

Do you have money? What do you have going for you to help you attain your goals and what do you need to get?

TASK 8.3

Set out your goals for the next five years. Pick one each in work, personal development and personal life. Do the same for yearly, quarterly, weekly and daily goals. Do your goals pass the tests above? Do you really want them? Keep a mini "goals book" and three times a day look at your goals list.

Review

Review both your goals and your performance on a regular basis. Do you still want the same things? Are you on target? What should you do differently in order to achieve your strategy?

OUTCOMES

Outcome / thinking

You need to decide your own personal goals and try, where possible, to ensure that these goals do not conflict with your business or work. You also need to consider the ecology of the situation. Is there any area of life in which making your goals happen could be adversely impacted? For instance, if you have a young family, and your goal is to travel and work abroad 28 days per month, this is unlikely to leave a lot of time for your family and will cause pressures / conflicts at home. This is why it is important to discuss your goals – both personal and business / work – with the key people in your life. Their support, or lack of it, will play a major part in whether you achieve your goals.

Outcome / orientation

In order to be more effective, you should always have an outcome orientation – that is, whatever you do, you should have thought ahead as to what result you want and acted accordingly. If you get on the phone to speak to a prospective customer, it is important that you are clear about what you want from the call. Perhaps you do not want, or expect, to make a sale over the phone; all you want from this phone call is to make an appointment for a face-to-face presentation. Therefore, you must ensure you do not try to sell your product / service too much over the phone and lose sight of your goal.

If you go to a networking event, what do you want to achieve? If you go and stay chatting to your best friend for the whole evening, you have failed. Much better to have reviewed the guest list and set yourself a realistic target of meeting four new people, including perhaps two people who might be customers for your company.

Thinking, even for a moment, about what you want to achieve tends to focus your mind on the key things and makes it less likely that you will waste time and lose focus on what should be the possible outcome. Meetings are famous for people getting drawn into discussions about irrelevant issues and things going off on a tangent. It is the chairman's responsibility to keep to an agenda. However, it is up to you as an individual attending the meeting to have your own outcome focus, to ensure you get what you want to achieve from attendance.

In each situation, prepare yourself by answering these questions:

- What positive outcome do you want?
- When specifically?
- What resources do you need to gather to achieve it?
- How will you know you have achieved this outcome?
- When will you review the outcome?

There is a strong correlation between being results-orientated and taking action. Focusing on outcomes is a 20 / 80 activity that will increase the likelihood of you taking appropriate action.

You may be a little worried that you will be seen as one of those people who "always has an angle", where people, particularly in your personal life, will come to assume that every seemingly innocent conversation or action has a purpose or hidden agenda. You do need to switch off at times but, to maintain work / life balance, the enterprising person needs to be making things happen and therefore, particularly in business, does not want to waste valuable opportunities presented at conferences, business meetings or negotiations.

Action overrated

I find it really hard to know when the outcome-setting ends and the action begins and *vice versa*. This is because outcome-setting without action is a complete waste of time but, similarly, doing things for the sake of it is equally so. I am sure you have heard Einstein's definition of insanity: "doing the same thing over and over again, expecting to achieve a different result".

Focused action is the key, but outcomes and action are part of that seamless loop discussed earlier where outcomes are set, action taken, feedback monitored and action taken, possibly of a different nature, to keep driving to achieve the initial outcomes.

There is no doubt that we are discussing the second key feature of enterprising behaviour. We have talked about being creative, curious and innovative to identify opportunities. Action is the other feature in the equation. Sadly, a lot of people do not take action, even when a golden opportunity is present. Why? Let's discuss this.

Why do people not take action?

First, without goals or outcomes, it is difficult to take any appropriate action. However, there are a whole host of other reasons, many of which have been discussed in detail in this book – for example:

- Belief: Lack of belief means you feel that whatever you do will not work.

- Personal mastery: Lack of confidence and negative emotions, such as fear of rejection or failure, also are inhibiting factors.

- Assertion: People lack assertion skills to state what they want and take action.

By working on these E-Factor skills, you will increase your chances of taking action. It is always easy to get into negative habits, such as procrastination, and that is why it is recommended that, once you have set a goal, you take a first small step towards the goal – for example:

- Desire: You may think you want the goal you have stated. Many people, when asked to state a goal, say they want to be a millionaire. If presented with a process or blueprint to achieve this goal, most will say, yes, they would like the money but not enough to be prepared to go outside their comfort zone. Taking action and being proactive usually involves getting out of your comfort zone and many people are just not prepared to do this unless they are pushed.

TASK 8.4

What do you want to change in your life? Are you prepared to do something about it? Face facts.

Inability to think strategically

Many of us are a bit like Pavlov's dogs – provided we receive immediate reward or reinforcement on taking action, we are keen to do so. You must realise that there are some steps to take that will make a difference in the long run. There are often activities that are important but not urgent but which will have an impact in the long run.

Paralysis analysis
Many highly-educated people, both academics and professionals, are capable of analysing an opportunity and of identifying all the problems of a new project. The problem is that, the more you do this, the better you get at it – just like anything else you practice. And then you become so good at identifying problems that the only things you see are problems! However, new projects / opportunities always have uncertainties and problems and part of the core skill of the enterprising person is that, once they have done their homework and overall feel comfortable with the calculated risk, they go for it!

Northern Ireland, where I come from, has one of the best enterprise support networks and one of the best educational systems in the UK. However, we also have one of the lowest rate of start-ups, particularly amongst women. InvestNI, the local regional development agency, has had to go so far as to spend significant funding on a promotional campaign urging the population as a whole to "Go for it". By providing road shows, role models, etc., InvestNI hopes to change the region's culture, by making people aware both of the help they need and its availability.

However, much more focus is needed on improving action orientation for individuals. I feel that too much education and training for entrepreneurs is awareness training and the provision of information. Personally, I feel action learning should play a bigger part in enterprise education and that students or trainers should actually do things. For example, practising the behaviour skills outlined within this book is much more likely to lead to the start of a new project rather than information on the tax system or analysing a case study. Ironically, many of the people who lead enterprise education courses have never actually started a new enterprise themselves – successfully or not – and, therefore, are advising others to go for something they haven't done themselves. They try to bring role models into the classroom, which helps, but, ultimately, enterprise action needs to be taught or mentored by people who have very direct real life experience to share.

The inner and outer enemy

Your inner critic will be one of your toughest opponents. You need to learn to override the fears that hold you back. Actually, it is that first or second step, no matter how small, that will help to lead to further action.

There is also jealousy in a lot of us, if we see someone doing something we would not dare to do. Instead of encouraging them and admiring them for their willingness to take action, there is almost a collective commitment to knock them for it and to hope secretly that it doesn't work for them, in order to justify our own position of inaction. This is the outer enemy.

So you can see there are lots of reasons why people don't take action. It is a lot easier to talk about doing something, or even to show somebody else how to do it, rather than to do it ourselves.

So how do we turn you into action man / woman?

As you can see, we can analyse why people don't take action ad infinitum. This is missing the point, as people will often find a new excuse to show why they never get round to things – it's amazing how creative people can be!

As someone who is actively involved in encouraging people to come up with business ideas, people never seize to amaze me. I have proved time and again that creativity is a learned skill and have been amazed by the quality of the ideas provided by the participants on my courses. It is not part of my remit to cajole them into turning the idea into reality but I think it is time I moved into this area. So many of them, having come up with an idea, barely consider even protecting the intellectual property.

One group of participants last November devised a new piece of equipment for the hospitality business. I then noticed the idea identified as a great opportunity in *The Sunday Times* business supplement. I went to see the group the next day, telling them to get down to the patent office, and explaining how highly the idea was rated. "Maybe after our exams in February", was their reply. Needless to say, the project never happened. It does not make this group of participants bad people; in fact, they were very nice. But, they represent the silent majority – all capable of coming up with great ideas / innovations but somehow never getting round to doing anything with them.

The steps

So what should you do to become more action-orientated?

1   The first thing I want you to do is that, every time you have a new idea, do something about it, no matter how small a step it is. If you want to start a new project, buy a book on it, make a phone call to get more information – start something!

2   Get a coach! A coach is not someone who advises you. A coach is someone who helps you plan your own action plan and then does everything in their power to make you carry it out. They will ring, email, meet, inspire and push. Sometimes, a paid coach is the answer, as your boss, bank manager, boyfriend / girlfriend or family member may be too involved to be detached. You may be lucky to have a role model who could act as a coach for you. But getting a coach, even for a short time, will boost your capability of taking action.

3   Keep your word – From now on, only agree to do something for somebody if you are 100% committed. If there is any uncertainty as to your commitment, then say "No". What you are doing is training yourself to keep your word to yourself, so that you understand that, when you say "Yes, I will do something", it is as good as done. This means a lot to customers, financiers, etc., and ensures your action orientation.

4   Chunk it down – break things into small manageable tasks and start doing this now with every project you take on.

5   Persist – Take action but be relaxed about the outcome. When obstacles appear, stop, draw breath, take action again and find a way round the obstacle.

6   Reward – Build your way up to increase self-motivation. If you need to do something you don't want to, give yourself a small immediate reward for taking action.

7   Find what drives you – If you are doing this for your family, remind yourself at least once a day why you are taking action now.

8   Start today – Remember there is no tomorrow. Ask yourself every day, what action have I taken towards my goals?

9   Always keep your plan goals to hand – Look at them everyday, at least once. You may only have five minutes free in the middle of all the fire-fighting. Use it for something, no matter how simple.

10 Get any form of support or help you can.

11 Work on your personal mastery – How do you see things? Do you see the project happening? Are you visualising it happening every day?

12 Seek out a like-minded person and support each other.

13 Time management – Leave time to take some action everyday and keep a journal (see the **Workbook & Journal** that accompanies this book).

14 Have weekly review sessions with yourself to monitor the process.

15 Learn self-discipline – Practise self-discipline. For instance, let's take exercise. Start off with five minutes' simple exercise every day. This doesn't seem much but, every day, you must make time for it. Build up gradually to 15 minutes every day. Not only will this help your health and energy but, again, you are playing games with your subconscious mind. You are showing it that you can have self-discipline and can make yourself do something every day, whether you want to or not. It doesn't matter what the focus is, it is more important that you are practising self-discipline. Some of you may have this quality already; for the rest of us, it is the unpleasant part of turning any idea into a reality. Constantly attack your comfort zones; if you are doing something that is an easy routine, find something different to do.

16 Task – List three comfort zones you have. Attack one of them.

17 Adopt a motto / affirmation – Use something like "just do it", or get yourself a paradigm that works for you, "I will take action", "I will make it happen", "action is the key". I was inspired to write this book and did so in less than a month, after reading Jeffrey Archer's prison journals. Strange you may say, but it was the fact that, despite the harsh prison

regime, Jeffrey Archer made himself get up at 5 o'clock every morning to write for two hours. Of all the traits, self-discipline is the one you must master. It is related to motivation but, where self-discipline kicks in is when the motivation to do something is not there but you still do what you have to do anyhow.

18 Find motivational aids – There may be a movie, a sporting event or a piece of music that motivates you – for example, I am rather partial to anything that reminds me of "Rocky". If you have got to take action, maybe do something that includes a confrontation you would rather avoid. Remember a role model who was able to confront a big problem. What would they do? How would they act?

19 Act confident – You may feel less than confident at times. However, moving confidently and acting confidently not only presents a confident stance to the outside world but also helps you to take action.

20 Find your own motivation strategy – It may be that you only really get moving when you are facing imminent disaster – lots of journalists only work when under the pressure of an imminent deadline. If that's the case, you need to visualise all the dire consequences that you will face if you do not take action. Sometimes, people wait until external circumstances create the need for action – better to create the circumstances yourself.

21 Keep an action journal – At the start of every day, ask yourself, "What three things will I do today to move my life forward?". At the end of every day, record faithfully whether you did anything towards achieving these three things.

22 Only get interested in profound knowledge – That is, knowledge that you can apply to your everyday life. If you are studying business strategy or attending a seminar on innovation, ask yourself, "What one idea from this lecture can I go and use now?".

23 People always say that information is power. However, information is only of any use if action is taken on it. If you sincerely want to develop your enterprise capability, you are on a mission to improve your ability to take action, otherwise known as personal power. Knowledge of a skill is no use, because it is not part of your normal behaviour. The only way to make it part of your normal behaviour is to start practising every day. Having a "do it now" attitude is good. You need to work on your E-

Factors daily. Practice the skills until they are part of you without thinking. To me, there is nothing more cruel than having knowledge or opportunity but a lifetime of inaction means that you let the opportunity slip by.

24 Work on your state – To get yourself into the action frame of mind. Usually, you will feel empowered in the right state, believing that you can do it now.

25 Model the people who take action – What is it about their beliefs, their thoughts and physiology that you could copy? Look at world leaders, but also look at successful local entrepreneurs or community leaders.

26 Be congruent – Make sure your voice, tonality, posture all match up.

27 You need energy. At times, you will have limited opportunity to take the action you need. If you are tired or run down, you will find it physically difficult to do what you know you should. Sensible diet, sleep and exercise patterns will help, together with working at relaxation so that stress will drain less of your energy away.

28 Listen to William Shakespeare in *The Merchant of Venice*, "If to do were as easy as to know what were good to do, chapels would be churches and poor men's cottages princes' palaces". Where you are now in life is a direct result of all the action you have taken (or not taken) to date. The chances are that, if you continue to take the same action, you will end up getting the same results. You need to realise that you may not always feel positive but you must continue to take positive action. Performing an act of random kindness can help. If someone is struggling with a shopping trolley, help them.

29 Limit your actions to the key 20% that make the difference. Don't waste your action muscles on unnecessary activity. Only take action where you can have an impact.

30 Take action on one area of your life at a time – Choose the area that is bothering you most. Find the key breakthrough things you must do and concentrate on them. Draw a schedule showing aim, action sequence and action start date.

31 Don't waste time, get into action. Every day you contemplate is a day wasted. Research and analysis is useful but you will learn from action that things happen, some good, some bad. If you can be flexible in your response, then you can take more appropriate action. The momentum

you create will open up opportunities for you. Time is your greatest resource. Every day you do not take focused action is a day wasted. The most successful entrepreneurs I have met were not necessarily workaholics. They used their time well; from 9 a.m. to 5 p.m., they took action, and they took the actions where they made the most impact, and then they enjoyed their private lives after that.

What three actions could you take now that could have the most leverage in your life? Do them today, not tomorrow. As is often said, anyone can do it. They can, if they set as their outcomes what they want from life at a macro and micro level and take focused action, respond where the desired result is not being immediately achieved and do something different if it will achieve a result.

A great enterprise person has the personal power to take action when it is necessary. Like a tiger on the prowl, they seem relaxed, watching what is happening; however, when the timing is right, they will put all their energy into positive focused attention.

Do it now! Don't delay. Always plan ahead. Look for what you want, then act on it, roll with the punches and keep taking action until your goals are achieved. Go for it!

Conclusion

So we have reached the end – or is it just the beginning? Perhaps it's both!

I hope you realise that you can be more enterprising and can improve your E-Factor, wherever you are now.

There are a few key things you must do to take the ideas you have looked at here and apply them to your life:

1   Decide which of the E-Factor competencies you need to work on.

2   Do something today!

3   Pick two ideas to work on.

4   Constantly search for opportunities to apply these competencies and skills, keep a journal and learn.

If you could just take one idea from each chapter and make it part of your life, you could make a massive change. Use the **Workbook & Journal** to help you work on your key E-Factors and to see the change in your world. You were born to be enterprising. It is time to do something about it. Do it now!

Appendix 1

Some thoughts on the Case study, Chapter 3

Jean needs to be enterprising if she is to set up a new project and to make it happen. Will she have to negotiate anything? Almost everything! For example:

1   First, she needs to agree the terms of her contract. Is it fixed term or permanent? What is her salary and benefits package?

2   Jean needs to agree with her boss exactly what outcomes have to be achieved and within what timescale.

3   Jean needs to establish what resources are available to her. Does she have a marketing budget? Does she have the help of any paid or volunteer staff?

4   Jean must negotiate some type of reward systems, if she completes the project successfully and on time.

5   Jean must do deals with local companies and give them some key benefit in return for their contribution in cash or kind.

6   Jean must design some type of deal for volunteers and look for negotiable benefits that might attract volunteers.

7   Jean must do deals with stakeholders at all stages of the projects.

8   Jean must identify alternative sources of funding and negotiate a package that could fund the operation pending corporate donations or fund-raising events.

9   Jean must look at what deals could bring in the £250,000 required and negotiate terms and conditions on each.

10 Jean must negotiate with friends and family to get their support in her new job.

Appendix 2

Jayne's Consultancy

Jayne has a serious cashflow problem, caused by expenditure in each of the first three months of trading without any income in those months. She needs at least £5,000 as an opening cash balance to correct this problem, or she needs to negotiate an overdraft of at least £5,000 with her bank manager.

Jayne's Consultancy: Cash budget for six months to (date)

Cash budget	M 1	M 2	M 3	M 4	M 5	M 6
	£	£	£	£	£	£
Income	0	0	0	2,000	3,000	2,000
Expenditure						
Costs	1,000	1,000	1,000	1,000	1,000	1,000
Salary	1,000	1,000	1,000	1,000	1,000	1,000
Total expenditure	**2,000**	**2,000**	**2,000**	**2,000**	**2,000**	**2,000**
Net cashflow	(2,000)	(2,000)	(2,000)	0	1,000	0
Opening cash balance	0	(2,000)	(4,000)	(6,000)	(6,000)	(5,000)
Net cash flow	(2,000)	(2,000)	(2,000)	0	1,000	0
Closing bank balance	(2,000)	(4,000)	(6,000)	(6,000)	(5,000)	(5,000)

Notes

About the StreetWise Guides

The StreetWise Guide to Being Enterprising has a companion **Workbook & Journal** (ISBN: 978-1-904887-32-4), which provides an assessment of your E-Factor skills, exercises to help you develop them over a 90-day period, a **Personal Journal** to record your development progress, and a further E-Factor questionnaire to evaluate your success in developing your enterprise skills.

You can find out more about the **StreetWise Guides** series at **www.streetwisecentral.com**.

About the Author

David A. Gibson is a law graduate and a chartered accountant. He is a senior lecturer in Enterprise at Queen's University, Belfast. He is also an entrepreneur, who has owned and led several enterprises. He is passionate about developing an enterprise culture and provides advice and support for start-up businesses (both private and social enterprise). His belief that enterprise skills can be taught has spilled over into other areas of outreach, including the public sector. He also works as a financial consultant, developing exit strategies for family-owned enterprises.

OAK TREE PRESS
is Ireland's leading business book publisher.

It develops and delivers
information, advice and resources
to entrepreneurs and managers –
and those who educate and support them.

Its print, software and web materials are in use in
Ireland, the UK, Finland, Greece, Norway, Slovenia,
India, Pakistan and Sri Lanka.

OAK TREE PRESS
19 Rutland Street
Cork, Ireland
T: + 353 21 4313855
F: + 353 21 4313496
E: info@oaktreepress.com
W: www.oaktreepress.com